PETER BOGDA
MOVIE OF TH

PETER BOGDANOVICH'S

MOVIE OF THE WEEK

52 CLASSIC FILMS FOR ONE FULL YEAR

BALLANTINE BOOKS • NEW YORK

A Ballantine Book
Published by The Ballantine Publishing Group

www.randomhouse.com/BB/

Library of Congress Cataloging-in-Publication Data
Bogdanovich, Peter, 1939–
Peter Bogdanovich's movie of the week.
p. cm.
Adapted from the author's column in
The New York Observer.
ISBN 0-345-43205-3 (pbk. : alk. paper)
1. Motion pictures Reviews. I. Title.
PN1995.B514 1999
791.43'75—dc21 99-28582

Cover design by David Stevenson
Cover photos © Archive Photos
Text design by Ann Gold

Manufactured in the United States of America

First Edition: November 1999
10 9 8 7 6 5 4 3 2 1

To three favorite women—my darling daughters,
Antonia Bogdanovich and Alexandra (Sashy) Bogdanovich,
and my dear wife, Louise Stratten—
with whom in aggregate I've certainly seen the most movies,
and who all have my undying love.

CONTENTS

*(A listing of complementary films concludes
each week's recommendations.)*

PETER BOGDANOVICH'S
MOVIE OF THE WEEK

Orson Welles (in white) as Charles Foster Kane gives his newspaper staff—Joseph Cotten (his right), Everett Sloane (his left)—an announcement that he's going to marry the president's niece in *Citizen Kane* (Week 18), cowritten, produced, and directed by Welles at age twenty-five.

Photo courtesy Photofest.

INTRODUCTION:
A YEAR OF CLASSICS

One time Orson Welles and I were talking about Greta Garbo. Welles adored her as an artist and was raving about her extraordinary presence, her mystery, her magic. I agreed. But wasn't it too bad, I said, that out of all the many films she'd appeared in, only two (George Cukor's *Camille* and Ernst Lubitsch's *Ninotchka*) were really good movies? Welles looked at me a long moment and then said, quietly: "You only need one. . . ."

Well, the majority of the filmmakers in this book—like the majority of the actors—are represented by only one film. My hope is that readers may be so intrigued by the one they read about, and then view, that they will search out the several others I've noted at the end of each recommendation—and thereby find themselves again in the presence of the same personality, the same aura.

Writing nearly all of these pieces (or their nucleus) on a weekly deadline for my column on the TV page of the iconoclastic *New York Observer*, I was decidedly at the mercy of what the next week's (uncut and uninterrupted) New York City television selections were to be. Usually I chose either the film I thought was best or the one about which I felt most impelled to write at that moment. Occasionally, if I had recommended one director's work over too many weeks, I would make another choice. Or if there was an arcane picture I thought wouldn't appeal to as many people, I would go instead for a more easily understandable or popular choice, because essentially I was writing not for film buffs but for an audience with a wider interest than movies and so with less time for the esoteric. Also, since it was primarily a New York audience, fewer Westerns (to which I'm partial) were chosen because I've found that this genre seems to be the least favorite among New Yorkers.

The idea for the form of this book came from my excellent editor at Ballantine, Associate Publisher Joe Blades, who suggested that organizing the pieces (with quite a few expanded and some new ones written) into a functional weekly cycle that spanned a year would give readers a useful structure they could follow—running a picture a week, with choices appropriate for certain holidays or celebrations. Joe also suggested that I attempt to include only films that are available for rental or purchase at video stores. The final list of movies, therefore, is by no means definitive. Nor do I think it in any way covers all the best pictures made— or even all my own personal favorites—although certainly a number of both are included.

Each of these movies is worth seeing at least once—and many of them, far more often. However, the overall book is not designed for diehard film buffs but rather for the intelligent general reader whose life does not revolve around movies, yet who might be interested in devoting a couple of hours every week to a classic or near-classic picture that still works for a contemporary audience, still has relevance and resonance.

The original notion of my writing these pieces came from Peter Kaplan, talented and resourceful editor in chief of Arthur Carter's enterprising *New York Observer;* Peter has my warmest gratitude for giving me a current voice in my hometown. (The last time I wrote about pictures on a regular basis was for a monthly column in *Esquire* in the early 1970s, though I did do a two-year weekly five-minute spot on older movies for *CBS News*'s national morning television show at the end of the Eighties.)

Apart from placing relevant pictures on certain dates—like John Ford's Irish comedy-romance, *The Quiet Man,* on St. Patrick's Day—my main objective was to hold the reader-viewer's interest from week to week, varying comedies, dramas, directors, stars, subjects in a flow that would be continually diverting and enjoyable. I've never been a big believer in art as medicine, something to be experienced "because it's good for you," though I definitely believe that quality work in any medium can be uplifting, healing, transforming. Obviously, some of these films are more challenging than others: *Singin' in the Rain* or *Bringing Up Baby* is easier to absorb than *Contempt* or *Ugetsu.* While many readers will skip around as they please, or ignore certain recommendations, the book has been designed for those who want to follow the suggested route.

The first pass at this material revealed obvious prejudices: I had six movies by Howard Hawks, six by John Ford, six by Ernst Lubitsch, six by Orson Welles, six by Jean Renoir. Over half of the year with five directors was not exactly a great idea for a general book of this kind (even if it might make me perfectly happy). My own predilections still being somewhat apparent, I've tried to give a far broader overview, and limited (to three or four) the number of films by the same director, so that now there are thirty-two directors of the fifty-two films (though Stanley Donen and Gene Kelly codirected their single entry).

Here's how the directors break down:

| Frank Capra | 2 | Charles Chaplin | 1 |
| John Cassavetes | 1 | George Cukor | 3 |

Stanley Donen	1	Kenji Mizoguchi	1
Allan Dwan	1	Otto Preminger	2
Blake Edwards	1	Carol Reed	1
John Ford	4	Jean Renoir	3
Jean-Luc Godard	1	Roberto Rossellini	1
Howard Hawks	4	Don Siegel	1
Alfred Hitchcock	3	Josef von Sternberg	1
Buster Keaton	1	George Stevens	1
Gene Kelly	1	Preston Sturges	3
Ernst Lubitsch	3	Frank Tashlin	1
Alexander Mackendrick	1	Jacques Tourneur	1
Elaine May	1	King Vidor	1
Leo McCarey	1	Raoul Walsh	1
Vincente Minnelli	2	Orson Welles	3

Unfortunately, this totally leaves out quite a few older filmmakers (not to mention the younger ones or my contemporaries) whose work I admire or cherish: Robert Aldrich, Ingmar Bergman, Budd Boetticher, Frank Borzage, Luis Buñuel, Claude Chabrol, René Clair, Roger Corman, Federico Fellini, Samuel Fuller, Tay Garnett, D. W. Griffith, John Huston, Chuck Jones, Stanley Kubrick, Akira Kurosawa, Gregory La Cava, Fritz Lang, David Lean, Jerry Lewis, Joseph H. Lewis, Harold Lloyd, Sidney Lumet, Anthony Mann, F. W. Murnau, Max Ophuls, Eric Rohmer, John Stahl, Jacques Tati, François Truffaut, Edgar G. Ulmer, Billy Wilder, and numerous others.

I also regret the lack of films with black stars or by black directors, and the inclusion of only one picture directed by a woman (Elaine May). But this I'm afraid fairly accurately reflects the minority situation in pictures of the past, only recently beginning to be remedied. In line with the interests of the general-audience majority to whom the book is addressed, there are also far fewer silent films and foreign films

Jean Renoir (left) as Octave, an
unemployed artist, with Carette
as an unemployed poacher, both
contemplating the complicated
and tragic conclusion to a
weekend of revelry in *The Rules
of the Game* (Week 48),
cowritten and directed by
Renoir at age forty-five.
Photo courtesy The Kobal Collection.

than I might prefer. Similarly, screenwriters, photographers, and other key credits are only occasionally specified.

Since stars have always been the main drawing card in pictures, a list of those included might be of interest. Although such brilliant American supporting players as William Demarest, Edward Everett Horton, Agnes Moorehead, and Eugene Pallette each appear twice, and the superb French characterman Marcel Dalio appears three times, only thirteen name actors herein are featured more than once.

The recurring stars are:

Ingrid Bergman	2	Maureen O'Hara	2
Joseph Cotten	4	Barbara Stanwyck	2
Cary Grant	7	James Stewart	3
Katharine Hepburn	3	Gene Tierney	2
Gene Kelly	2	John Wayne	2
Shirley MacLaine	2	Orson Welles	
Dean Martin	2	(including one narration)	4

All of the following appear in only one picture each, and a number of very important stars—Greta Garbo is a glaring example—are unfortunately not represented; however, there are certainly quite a number who are: Don Ameche, Judith Anderson, Dana Andrews, Eve Arden, Jean Arthur, Fred Astaire, Mary Astor, Lew Ayres, Lauren Bacall, Brigitte Bardot, John Barrymore, Wallace Beery, Eleanor Boardman, Humphrey Bogart, Charles Boyer, Eddie Bracken, James Cagney, Leslie Caron, Charlie Chaplin, Maurice Chevalier, Suzanne Cloutier, Claudette Colbert, Jackie Coogan, Gary Cooper, Dolores Costello, Donald Crisp, Tony Curtis, Marlene Dietrich, Kirk Douglas, Irene Dunne, Tom Ewell, Aldo Fabrizi, Douglas Fairbanks, Nina Foch, Henry Fonda, Pierre Fresnay, Jean Gabin, Clark Gable, Ben Gazzara, Farley Granger, Jane Greer, Rita Hayworth, Audrey Hepburn,

Judy Holliday, Tim Holt, Trevor Howard, Josephine Hull, Betty Hutton, Emil Jannings, Buster Keaton, Grace Kelly, Machiko Kyo, Burt Lancaster, Priscilla Lane, René Le-Fèvre, Oscar Levant, Jerry Lewis, Carole Lombard, Kevin McCarthy, Jeanette MacDonald, Roddy McDowall, Micheál Macliammóir, Anna Magnani, Dorothy Malone, James Mason, Raymond Massey, Walter Matthau, Elaine May, Virginia Mayo, Joel McCrea, Robert Mitchum, Frank Morgan, James Murray, Patricia Neal, Donald O'Connor, Jack Palance, George Peppard, Michel Piccoli, Walter Pidgeon, Vincent Price, Lee Remick, Jean Renoir, Debbie Reynolds, Ginger Rogers, Mickey Rooney, Gena Rowlands, Eva Marie Saint, George C. Scott, Frank Sinatra, Erich von Stroheim, Margaret Sullavan, Spencer Tracy, Rudy Vallee, Alida Valli, Robert Walker, Clifton Webb, Dana Wynter.

It will be noted that the heavy emphasis is on pictures made before the 1960s. One of several reasons for this is that I think there's a huge overemphasis in American culture on the new, and far too many younger filmgoers seem to think that movies began sometime in the Seventies or Eighties, and evince absolutely no interest in anything earlier. That Hollywood pictures overall have got progressively worse since the early 1960s—except for a brief renaissance almost a decade later—is a fact acknowledged and lamented by nearly every film critic and historian. The choices here are a small attempt to redress the balance and current topical emphasis, to give a hint of the vast treasures that (in our home-video age) are out there for the taking from the years roughly between 1920 and 1960, the true golden age of the movies. Of course, there were numerous superb films made before the Twenties and after the Sixties, but (I repeat) this book is in no way intended as an all-encompassing view.

Another undeniable reason for the preponderance of pictures of the 1940s and 1950s is that these are the years in which I was growing up, and I'm afraid that filmgoing affections connect unalterably to a person's own life (though this doesn't easily explain my fondness for the 1930s). Movies—as with all popular culture (perhaps as with all cultural events, as well as all other experiences in life)—are often anchored in memories of where we were and who we were with and what we were like when first exposed to them. There's no way around it: Even outright trash can achieve a special glow for someone if the person associates it with a happy time in his or her life. I was extremely fortunate that my father took me to silent pictures (at New York's Museum of Modern Art) when I was a child, so these essential founding blocks of the medium never seemed strange or distant. If you want to give your children a broader horizon in their lives, get them at a young age to see good pictures of far earlier decades than their own.

Anyway, here's a breakdown by decade of the films herein recommended:

1920s	4	1960s	4
1930s	11	1970s	1
1940s	18	1980s	1
1950s	13		

A couple of years ago, a brand-new 35mm print of Alfred Hitchcock's *North by Northwest* (see Week 32) was playing at a big-screen theater near my home. I hadn't seen it that way for close to thirty years, though I'd originally watched the picture in theaters five times in its first seven years. Since the start of the home-video age, I had seen the movie a couple of times and still enjoyed it, but not until seeing it again on the big screen did I realize conclusively what a gigantic difference screen size does make. I was instantly reminded of my dear mother's remark that the difference between seeing a film on a theater screen as opposed to television was like the difference between seeing a painting on a wall and looking at a reproduction of it in a book. Behind this may be yet another reason why younger people have a hard time with older pictures: They've only seen them on the tube, and that reduces films' mystery and mythic impact.

In my earliest Manhattan days of serious movie talk, if you'd seen a film exclusively on TV, we just used to say you hadn't really seen it at all. What can we do about this today? There are now fewer and fewer revival houses, more and more ways of seeing pictures at home. But there simply is no way to duplicate the wonderfully dreamlike, yet communal, experience of a theater screening: a live audience, a large screen, a good 35mm print. After only nine months even the biggest hit of recent years, *Titanic,* could be seen only on the small screen. I don't really see a solution to this huge cultural dilemma, except to push for the funding of large-scale revival houses in every major city, with an increasing supply of new prints of classic films.

After all, it's only movies that are commonly referred to as "old." Nobody says, "Have you read that old book by Dostoyevsky?" or "Seen that old painting by Rembrandt?" or "Heard that old symphony by Mozart?" or "Seen that old play by Shakespeare?" If you have not seen a movie, it is new. Yes, certainly many films date badly (as do many books, symphonies, paintings, and plays). But many do not date at all. Even though their makers and their casts may all have died, the work can remain forever fresh and young, eternally new, profoundly rewarding.

"I'd walk home," says Lauren
Bacall as Slim in this scene from
Howard Hawks's *To Have and
Have Not* (Week 4), "if it wasn't
for all that water." Later,
Humphrey Bogart (as Harry,
whom she calls Steve) insolently
mimics the line back to show a
certain lack of trust. Out of
Hemingway, via Faulkner.
Photo courtesy Photofest.

AN AMERICAN IN PARIS

There's nothing like a solid musical to start the year with a smile.

The tricky thing about musicals, though, is that if they're really good, they look easy. Yet there is nothing tougher to pull off, as such contemporary filmmakers as Martin Scorsese, Francis Coppola, Woody Allen, and notoriously yours truly have learned to our (and our backers') considerable cost. The genre demands the right songs, their correct integration, the perfect balance between musical numbers and dialogue, the suspension of disbelief required to get away with singing and dancing in nonbackstage stories, and, above everything, the performing talents to make it all work effortlessly.

It's no coincidence that the best and the most popular picture musicals have clustered around a precious few gifted personalities like Maurice Chevalier, Fred Astaire, Ginger Rogers, Judy Garland, Bing Crosby, Gene Kelly, Frank Sinatra, Jerry Lewis, Dean Martin, Elvis Presley, Barbra Streisand, and Liza Minnelli. So many song and dance numbers—especially in the finest musicals of the past, starting with the great first one, Ernst Lubitsch's *The Love Parade* (1929) starring Chevalier and a sweet, sexy Jeanette MacDonald, and onward through the Astaire-Rogers series of the 1930s, to the various Gene Kelly collaborations of the late 1940s and 1950s—were done in long continuous takes, and only performers with chops at their tops can do that. All the earliest musicals were done with the orchestra right off camera, recording singers, sound effects, and all the instruments at exactly the same time, which gives the five Lubitsch musicals a great part of their charm, their absolute sense of true immediacy (see Week 49).

While the Lubitsch musicals set the standard for quality, the more proletarian Astaire and Rogers shows were far more popular (see Week 17). But Gene Kelly was at the heart of what became known as the modern movie musical, both setting the standard and achieving great popularity.

At the time, the apogee was thought to be the 1951 Academy Award–winner as best picture of the year, *An American in Paris,* achieved by an amazing group of now legendary musical talents: director Vincente Minnelli, choreographer and star Gene Kelly, screenwriter Alan Jay Lerner, producer Arthur Freed, costars Oscar Levant and Georges Guétary and new discovery Leslie Caron, lyricist Ira Gershwin—and all music by George Gershwin, for God's sake! The subject matter? An American painter in Paris has two loves—one his patron (a quality nonmusical performance by Nina Foch), the other his soul mate (Ms. Caron), who has a patron lover, too (M. Guétary). The movie features a twenty-minute ballet at the end as a kind of grand Impressionist period daydream, with paintings by Renoir, Cezanne, Toulouse-Lautrec, and Gauguin coming to life.

Even my father—a European painter and concert pianist born in the last year of the last century (like Alfred Hitchcock), very much influenced by the French, and an intellectual of the Parisian Twenties, who listened only to the finest classical music and therefore generally had no interest in or affection for American musicals—liked *An American in*

Paris. He also used to say Gershwin was the one great American popular composer, a fine musician. Certainly his tunes seem to wear the best, and his brother Ira's lyrics are at the summit of a medium in which Americans excelled. When I was younger, while I liked *An American in Paris*, I preferred the Kelly–Stanley Donen collaborations (like Week 25's *Singin' in the Rain*) or the Astaire-Minnelli *The Band Wagon*, and I still love them. But I must say, on more recent viewings, *An American in Paris* is looking awfully good. Kelly's choreography and his own dancing are at their classiest, yet most poignantly exuberant. And those songs! Every one a classic of its kind: "I Got Rhythm," "By Strauss," "Stairway to Paradise," "Our Love Is Here to Stay."

Yes, Oscar Levant was no great actor, and his one number, where he plays all the instruments in the orchestra (a bit stolen from a 1921 Buster Keaton two-reeler, *The Playhouse,* where Buster was every actor and even the audience— a light metaphoric send-up of Charlie Chaplin's taking credit for every aspect of his films), is not the best, and yes, the script is short on laughs. But there is a knowing air of melancholy about the compromises of love that brings an unexpected depth to the lyric passages, like the pas de deux under the Seine bridge for "Our Love Is Here to Stay" that is transfixing in its romantic loveliness. The concluding ballet is the absolute best of its kind in pictures, better than any of the others Kelly did that preceded it (starting with *On the Town*) or any that followed, including one satiric imitation by Astaire (in *The Band Wagon*). A large plus here, naturally, is Gershwin's constantly surprising music, but Kelly's choreography is really terrific.

Anyone who contributes to musical comedy hits in the Broadway theater on the level Gene Kelly did should be able to live off his royalties forever. But I remember Gene in his last decades (he died in 1996) telling me with sad eyes—when asked how it felt being a part of pictures with such continuing appeal as *Singin' in the Rain*, *On the Town*, and *An American in Paris*—that it was great, but did I realize he received not one red cent from any of the video or television sales his classics generated? All he ever got was that weekly MGM salary while he was working.

This is one of the reasons why the star system ended and why the stars took out their vengeance on the studios that had exploited them. The result is that now stars' pay has become obscene—and the studios are totally at their mercy. Well, two wrongs don't make a right.

Nevertheless, Gene's spirit will always be with us, and in *An American in Paris* he dances out for us the beauty and heartbreak behind great love and great loss. He portrays an American artist who had been a soldier or sailor (which Kelly had played popularly in *On the Town*, and to an Oscar nomination for best actor in *Anchors Aweigh*) and helped to liberate Paris from the Nazis, had saved its beauty for the world, but at great cost. *An American in Paris* was the climax of American postwar optimism with a sense of tragic recent events, so that to sing or dance in freedom by the river Seine meant more than a clever number. And this feeling, which was in the wind of the times, is here memorialized in movement: when Gene Kelly dances the polka with a rotund French lady in an indoor/outdoor café, or tap-dances out on the free sidewalks of lovely Paris to the visible utter delight of twenty adorable children.

In romantic, or mythic, movie terms, this was the same Paris of love that only eight years before (in *Casablanca*) Humphrey Bogart and Ingrid Bergman had said they would always have; and Gene helped to save it, and danced for them, too! See the all-positive American aura that America and the world embraced in 1951, and see from what a high we have fallen. But pictures bring back that spirit, which is a big deal, and should be on the big screen, where its mythic size can properly counteract the pygmy dynamites of today. Failing that, sit close to the largest big-screen TV and enjoy two hours of American happy times, just a breath away from the encroaching darkness of Korea, the sexual revolution, drugs, the victory of TV, at least three earth-shattering assassinations, and Vietnam. In fact, all the most enduring postwar musicals were made in exactly that brief five-year period (1949–1954). Happily, all these movies are readily available today. See America's last innocent moment and cry for joy.

ANOTHER VINCENTE MINNELLI–GENE KELLY MUSICAL:
  The Pirate (1948; with Judy Garland, Walter Slezak; songs by Cole Porter).

OTHER MUSICALS DIRECTED BY MINNELLI:
  Cabin in the Sky (1943; with Ethel Waters, Lena Horne, Louis Armstrong).
  Meet Me in St. Louis (1944; with Judy Garland).
  The Band Wagon (1953; with Fred Astaire, Cyd Charisse).
  Gigi (1958; with Leslie Caron, Maurice Chevalier).
  Bells Are Ringing (1960; with Judy Holliday, Dean Martin).

THE LADY EVE

Still in that New Year's mood . . . There's never been a better title for a romantic comedy with screwball overtones than the one Preston Sturges came up with for what is also certainly high among the ten best ever made in my favorite genre. *The Lady Eve* may be Sturges's best, too, which is saying a lot, since he made several that were terrific. This is the one in which Henry Fonda, at age thirty-five, plays an ale-heir millionaire who studies snakes and, after a long while in the jungle, finds himself on an ocean liner with the sexiest, smartest, most attractive cardsharp–con artist you could ever imagine, played by Barbara Stanwyck at age thirty-three.

It was only Sturges's third film as a director-writer—one of the first such hyphenates in American talking-picture history, whose extraordinary success opened the door for the scores who've followed—but the third in an amazing eight-films-in-four-years (1940–1944) streak of creative energy and brilliance unparalleled in U.S. movies. In fact, that same memorable year, 1941, saw the release of another Sturges masterwork, his so-called testament film—in which the picture-maker defines cinema for himself—an oddball romantic comedy-drama-satire of Hollywood, *Sullivan's Travels*.

The Lady Eve is also the single time in Henry Fonda's long and valuable career that he played this sort of absent-minded innocent-professor type, or did the kind of slapstick-pratfall business he does repeatedly here, and with such wonderful enthusiasm that you'd think he would have made a specialty of these roles. If you doubt Fonda's range, compare the work for Sturges with his Abe Lincoln (in John Ford's *Young Mr. Lincoln*, 1939), or with his Tom Joad (in Ford's *The Grapes of Wrath*, 1940), which just preceded it. *The Lady Eve* is Stanwyck's best comedy, too, and she is so good in it, you forget she was equally brilliant at drama. Actually, in 1941, not only was her other top comedy released—Howard Hawks's *Ball of Fire* with Gary Cooper, cowritten by Billy Wilder—but also one of her finest dramatic performances, with Cooper again, in Frank Capra's *Meet John Doe* (see Week 27).

The supporting cast is also of such remarkable quality you realize how much actors like these had to do with the richness and complexity of pictures in the golden age. Charles Coburn, for example, as Stanwyck's cardsharp–con-artist dad, brings great dignity to his role, and portly Eugene Pallette is hilarious as Fonda's incredulous father. William Demarest was in nearly all of Sturges's films and you can see why: tough character-men who can be funny just don't come any better.

Exhilaratingly fast-paced and surprisingly complicated, *The Lady Eve* has numerous snakelike twists, and the sophisticated moral view that emerges is also neither predictable nor easy, as it never was in Sturges's best work. The dame may be wrong, but the guy turns out to be more wrong until he learns his lesson: the battle of the sexes is an uneven one in many ways—women having the advantage over the long haul. Cary Grant once summed it up to me succinctly: "The women always win in the end, you know, so you might as well just give in early." This attitude, of course, could stand as a wonderful Sturges trademark. The key line in the movie is Stanwyck's to the effect that the "good" girls aren't always as good as they seem, and the "bad" ones aren't as bad, "not nearly as bad": a valid comment on most people in general.

OTHER PRESTON STURGES COMEDIES:

The Great McGinty (1940; with Brian Donlevy, Akim Tamiroff).

Christmas in July (1940; with Dick Powell, Gail Patrick).

Sullivan's Travels (1941; with Joel McCrea, Veronica Lake).

Also see Weeks 10 and 40.

THE AWFUL TRUTH

January 16 is Cary Grant's birthday and, as you might guess from the number of times his films appear in this book—seven, with five directors—Grant was my favorite leading man. It is appropriate then to celebrate his birth in life with his birth in pictures—his movie-star birth—if by no means his debut. He had already appeared in no less than twenty-eight films—only about five worth seeing—when he became an A-list actor in the other romantic screwball comedy (besides Sturges's *The Lady Eve*) with a perfect title for the genre, Leo McCarey's scintillating 1937 classic, *The Awful Truth*.

The brilliantly urbane McCarey—the man who in the silent era had put Stan Laurel with Oliver Hardy—won the Academy Award as best director (a prize rarely given to comedy) for this, and his coaching of Grant (who, it is said, closely emulated McCarey's dry, sophisticated demeanor) resulted in the actor's first starring success and no doubt his most defining role. The movie was also nominated for best picture (McCarey produced) and best screenplay (by Viña Delmar, with much improvisation on the set by McCarey), with best actress and best supporting actor nominations going to Irene Dunne and Ralph Bellamy. Dunne is at her absolute wittiest and is extremely winning, and Bellamy is the squarest-ever Oklahoman "other man."

As in *The Lady Eve*, the guy is the one who must learn the lessons of true love, and so the film reminds us again that women on the American screen once had a strong and often morally superior voice. Right in the first scene we find out that Grant has not told his wife the truth—he has *not* been to Florida—but rather seems to have been up to some kind of hanky-panky (what-she-doesn't-know-won't-hurt-her department). Coming home, he finds her gone. Soon after, when she returns from an overnight with her singing coach in what looks like a compromising situation, it is clear she's telling the truth about the innocence of the adventure she has endured. But Cary is actually quite guilty himself. He gives her an orange without noticing that it has CALIFORNIA stamped on it, and when she calls him on this, he gets on his high horse about her "escapade." This leads to a divorce.

And from here on, the big question is how these two—obviously in love with each other—will ever get to the "awful truth" and reconcile. Dunne goes out with Bellamy and endures his suspicious and protective mother; Grant starts dating—first a showgirl, then a rich society woman.

The mix-ups and mismatchings accelerate in one hilarious sequence after another: a scene with two identical derby hats and a very clever dog; Bellamy enthusiastically singing "Home on the Range"; a jealous Grant barging in on a recital Dunne is giving. A classic scene plays in a nightclub, where Grant and his showgirl end up at a table with Dunne and Bellamy; Irene tells Cary she's going to marry Ralph and move to Oklahoma City. Grant congratulates them. "And just think," he says, "if you ever get bored, you can always go up to *Tulsa* for the weekend!" The final two sequences are memorable: Dunne pretends to be Grant's ultravulgar sister and breaks up a high-toned society do, and then the pair end up in adjoining rooms in a rustic inn, separated only by one door and a stubborn cat. . . .

Certainly among the great American comedies, this remains as remarkably fresh and buoyant as ever—more so. It has, too, an adult kind of witty sophistication that is perfectly representative of the best aspects of the glorious Thirties. How did we ever get so dumbed down to the prevalent sophomoric humor of the Nineties?

The Awful Truth is perhaps the supreme example of light comedy that's also real, human, and mature in dealing with man's often frivolous idiosyncrasies and foolishness.

ANOTHER LEO McCAREY–CARY GRANT–IRENE DUNNE PICTURE:
> *My Favorite Wife* (1940; with Randolph Scott; conceived and produced by McCarey; directed by Garson Kanin).

OTHER McCAREY-GRANT PICTURES:
> *Once Upon a Honeymoon* (1942; with Ginger Rogers, Walter Slezak).
> *An Affair to Remember* (1957; with Deborah Kerr).

ANOTHER McCAREY-DUNNE PICTURE:
> *Love Affair* (1939; with Charles Boyer).

OTHER McCAREY COMEDIES:
> *Duck Soup* (1933; with the Marx Brothers).
> *Six of a Kind* (1934; with W. C. Fields, George Burns, Gracie Allen).
> *Belle of the Nineties* (1934; with Mae West).
> *Ruggles of Red Gap* (1935; with Charles Laughton).
> *Going My Way* (1944; with Bing Crosby, Barry Fitzgerald).
> *The Bells of St. Mary's* (1945; with Bing Crosby, Ingrid Bergman).
> *Rally 'Round the Flag, Boys!* (1958; with Paul Newman, Joanne Woodward, Joan Collins).

TO HAVE AND HAVE NOT

On a fishing trip in the early 1940s, Howard Hawks told Ernest Hemingway that he could make a good movie out of the author's worst book. "Which one was that?" Hemingway asked irritably, and Hawks replied, "That bunch of junk called *To Have and to Have Not*." (Hawks thought so little of the book that he always said the title wrong, adding the extra *to*.) Supposedly, Hemingway protested that it was not possible to make a movie of this potboiler, but Hawks insisted that he could, and the two spent the next ten days fishing and discussing the characters in the novel and how they had met before the book's story began.

This "prequel" became the premise for an essentially new work, set no longer in Cuba but in Martinique, and very loosely inspired by certain events and characters in the novel—in other words, an original screenplay with contributions from two or three more writers, including Hawks himself and William Faulkner. This was the only artistic association between these two American literary giants, though Faulkner and Hemingway never actually worked together; it was always through Hawks. The resultant 1944 movie, starring Humphrey Bogart and introducing Lauren Bacall, is probably the best love-story-and-foreign-intrigue picture ever made. In the same genre, I much prefer *To Have and Have Not* to the more famous *Casablanca*,

and I watch it more often, not least because it has a happy ending.

Hawks had been trying for years to create "an American Marlene Dietrich," first with Frances Farmer (in the first half of his 1936 *Come and Get It*), then sporadically with both Jean Arthur and Rita Hayworth (in his 1939 *Only Angels Have Wings*; see Week 24). But Hawks didn't hit the mark until he found and then carefully molded teenage fashion model Lauren Bacall. Sending her out to the desert to shout Shakespeare into the wind, Hawks broke Ms. Bacall's voice to the husky tones of Dietrich and gave her unafraid, impertinent lines, which he had found Bacall could deliver without losing likability.

The director's skill with the newcomer and the careful way he dressed and photographed her were enhanced by an accident of fate no one could have predicted, though Hawks must have realized he was playing with fire by confronting Bogart, the most insolent star of the screen, with a character expressly created to equal and even trump the actor's screen persona. The upshot was that Bogart, a married man in his mid-forties, fell madly in love with his nineteen-year-old costar, and she with him. As Hawks said, this naturally made it easier for him to direct all those scenes Bacall stole from Bogie.

Whichever way you look at it, the chemistry between "Bogie and Baby" (as they were immediately dubbed in the press) is so palpable, it photographs in spades. Unique in movie history, the mythic affection played on two levels at once and was captured fresh, so to speak, as it was magically happening both inside and outside the fiction. It is so strong in *To Have and Have Not* that I think never before or since has romantic yet earthy love so apparently and joyously triumphed against the world. Endings don't get much more cheerful than Bacall's final exit, Bogart holding her arm, and she wiggling her hips happily to the Hoagy Carmichael music.

Naturally, the real-life affair and subsequent marriage of Bacall and Bogart helped to make the film a box-office smash, leading to the quick follow-up teaming of the pair in Hawks's version of Raymond Chandler's first Philip Marlowe novel, *The Big Sleep* (1946); here the two are again terrific, but in a more settled, less electric way. When Hawks finally showed *To Have and Have Not* to Marlene Dietrich, she supposedly said, "You son of a bitch—that's me fifteen years ago." And Hawks answered, "Yes, and in another fifteen years we'll do it with somebody else"—which he actually did do, in a much softer way, with Angie Dickinson in *Rio Bravo* (1959).

The two most archetypal Bogart films, in fact, are *To Have and Have Not* and *The Big Sleep*, and this is not surprising considering Hawks's extraordinary ability to define a star's persona—whether that star was Bogart, John Wayne, Gary Cooper, Cary Grant, or Marilyn Monroe. The Hemingway-based picture features lovely supporting performances from jazzy singer and "Stardust" songwriter Hoagy Carmichael as the café pianist Cricket, and Marcel Dalio, one of Jean Renoir's stars from *Grand Illusion* and *The Rules of the Game* (see Weeks 16 and 48), as Frenchy, the café's owner. One of my favorite lines: as Dalio, tears in his eyes, moves to Bogart to thank him from the bottom of his heart for risking his own life, Bogie says, "Don't kiss me, Frenchy"—an *echt* Hawks line if there ever was one.

Walter Brennan is both funny and touching as Bogart's closest friend, a rummy who "used to be good." The truthfulness and complexity of this relationship grounds the picture and makes more real the romanticism. Note the differences and similarities in relationships in other Hawks pictures, such as Thomas Mitchell's "Kid" and Cary Grant's

"Pop" in *Only Angels Have Wings*. A nonstop exciting masterpiece of atmosphere and character, *To Have and Have Not* is one of my own personal favorites.

ANOTHER HOWARD HAWKS–HUMPHREY BOGART–LAUREN BACALL PICTURE:
  The Big Sleep (1946).

OTHER HAWKS PICTURES:
  The Crowd Roars (1932; with James Cagney, Joan Blondell).
  The Big Sky (1952; with Kirk Douglas, Dewey Martin).
  Rio Bravo (1959; with John Wayne, Angie Dickinson, Dean Martin, Ricky Nelson, Walter Brennan).
  Hatari! (1962; with John Wayne, Elsa Martinelli).
  El Dorado (1967; with John Wayne, Robert Mitchum).

Also see Weeks 24, 29, and 42.

Spencer Tracy is prosecutor in the attempted-murder case against Judy Holliday (center), and Katharine Hepburn is her defense lawyer, but outside the courtroom, Tracy and Hepburn are married (!) in George Cukor's hilarious battle of the sexes, *Adam's Rib* (Week 7), from a brilliant script by Ruth Gordon and Garson Kanin.

Photo courtesy The Kobal Collection.

ANATOMY OF A MURDER

In 1959—when Frank Sinatra and Elvis Presley and Marilyn Monroe were red-hot—one of the finest and most important American films was released, did well, won an award or two (like the New York Film Critics' selection of James Stewart as best actor), and then passed from the scene. But it should be required viewing for anyone who cares about true quality in picture-making, America's complicated judicial system, and life's generally ambiguous pathways. Costarring Lee Remick, Ben Gazzara (in only his second film), George C. Scott (in his first big role), Arthur O'Connell, Eve Arden, and the national hero Joseph N. Welch (the man who brought down Joe McCarthy) as the judge, the film is Otto Preminger's enthralling adaptation of Robert Traver's bestseller founded on a true story of rape, murder, and the subsequent courtroom trial.

That Robert Traver is a pseudonym for the actual defendant's lawyer in this case, that the entire movie was shot on the real locations in upper Michigan where the events took place, and that Preminger was first trained as a lawyer—his father having been attorney general of Austria and one of its most famous attorneys—help to give *Anatomy of a Murder* its pervasive feeling of truth. Stewart gives a performance of absolutely perfect pitch. Though he was among the top five stars of the Fifties, *Anatomy* was the peak in popularity for

his career and one of the last roles of significance he was to
have. All the other performances, down to the bits, are right
up there with Stewart's, the movie being a seamless blend-
ing and contrast of young and older star actors—a Preminger trademark at its zenith.

Indeed, one could say that each of the leading actors is
here given his or her most defining role: Eve Arden as Stewart's wisecracking secretary; Lee Remick as the somehow innocently sexy all-American tease; Ben Gazzara as the edgy,
suppressed volcano of anger, resentment, sarcasm; Arthur
O'Connell as the lovable and wise old Irish drunk; George C.
Scott as the arrogant, marble-smooth, diabolically clever
city lawyer. All these are working at such a high level that
together they attain the kind of mythic size Preminger
clearly had in mind: they are recognizably human yet archetypes as well.

Preminger's best and most personal film, *Anatomy* also
features a unique, utterly fresh score, one of only two ever
composed by the peerless, innovative, incomparable Duke
Ellington, who even appears briefly in a piano bar with
Stewart. (Jimmy was so enraptured with Ellington's music
that he would stay up at night in the hotel bar until
way past the actor's necessary—because of early morning
shooting—bedtime, and Preminger had to put his foot
down and forbid the playing.)

The picture also had a tremendous impact on the freedom of the screen. After getting taboo words like *virgin*
and *pregnant* into his otherwise innocuous *The Moon Is
Blue* (1953), and being the one finally to address drug
addiction—with Sinatra in probably his most powerful dramatic performance—in *The Man with the Golden Arm*
(1955), Preminger dealt Hollywood's Production Code the
coup de grâce with *Anatomy*, as America's own Jimmy Stewart uses words like *penetration, panties,* and *spermatogenesis.*

Indeed, accepting the role was a measure of Stewart's artistic conscience. Though many of his heartland fans objected to what they saw, Stewart told me once there was no way he "could turn down a part as good as that." The theme of the movie, most eloquently spoken by Stewart, that people are neither all good nor all bad is worth remembering daily.

OTHER OTTO PREMINGER DRAMAS:

The Man with the Golden Arm (1955; with Frank Sinatra, Kim Novak).

Bonjour Tristesse (1958; with David Niven, Jean Seberg, Deborah Kerr).

Exodus (1960; with Paul Newman, Eva Marie Saint, Sal Mineo, Lee J. Cobb, Ralph Richardson).

Advise and Consent (1962; with Henry Fonda, Charles Laughton, Walter Pidgeon).

The Cardinal (1963; with John Huston, Tom Tryon, Carol Lynley).

In Harm's Way (1965; with John Wayne, Kirk Douglas, Patricia Neal).

Hurry Sundown (1967; with Michael Caine, Jane Fonda).

Also see Week 46.

WHITE HEAT

In 1970—a decade before the videocassette age—Orson Welles had rented a house for a year in Beverly Hills, and one evening I brought over a portable 16mm projector so that we could run a print I'd borrowed of James Cagney at his annihilating best in Raoul Walsh's amazing 1949 gangster picture, *White Heat.* Both Orson and I had seen the movie before and we both remembered it as being one of Walsh's and one of Cagney's finest, most exciting, and memorable; that night confirmed this for us. Orson, of course, was quite vocally delighted by the film's extraordinarily subversive qualities.

Here is Cagney at his most savagely antisocial, a psychopathic, chronically migrained, aging mama's-boy train-robbing killer named Cody Jarrett. And yet when that most honorable Federal undercover agent Edmond O'Brien bullshits his way into the gang, you are rooting for Cagney all the way. Welles and I were actually hissing O'Brien! Which made Orson laugh—happy with the film's relentlessly perverse effect: because of Cagney's hypnotic, charismatic personality and his sheer brilliance as an actor, Law and Order is undercut and a kind of breathtaking anarchy becomes almost alluring—if it weren't so terrifying underneath.

Raoul Walsh was one of the five directors he had worked with whom Cagney characterized as "a *real* director."

Which was what? I asked. And Cagney said: "A real director is a guy who, if I don't know what the hell to do, can get up and show me!" Walsh had been a fine silent actor as well (see him in his own production of *Sadie Thompson*, 1928, with Gloria Swanson), so Cagney, confident of being in great hands, gives by far his most daring performance. The section when he goes berserk in the prison mess, having heard of his mother's death, is absolutely hair-raising. A number of people have commented on Walsh's being the only conceivable director who could have Cagney sit on his mother's lap and get away with it. In fact, the move seems absolutely organic to the character.

British actress Margaret Wycherly as Cody Jarrett's deadpan, whiskey-voiced mother is a marvel herself. Not to mention Virginia Mayo as the ultimate gun moll incarnate and Steve Cochran equally definitive as her oily hunk of a lover. And when Cagney commits suicide rather than give up—standing cockily on that gigantic globelike gas tank, in a field of gas tanks, shooting directly into it, yelling, "Top o' the world, Ma!" just before his world blasts into smithereens—it is among the most ambiguously thrilling moments in movie history. *White Heat* both revived Warner Brothers' gangster cycle of the Thirties and also ended it conclusively for the golden age, which still had about thirteen years to go. In other words, this is the climax of the gangster genre.

OTHER RAOUL WALSH–JAMES CAGNEY PICTURES:
> *The Roaring Twenties* (1939; with Humphrey Bogart, Priscilla Lane).
> *The Strawberry Blonde* (1941; with Rita Hayworth, Olivia de Havilland).
> *A Lion Is in the Streets* (1953; with Barbara Hale, Anne Francis).

OTHER WALSH GANGSTER-ACTION PICTURES:

They Drive by Night (1940; with George Raft, Humphrey Bogart, Ida Lupino).

High Sierra (1941; with Humphrey Bogart, Ida Lupino).

Pursued (1947; with Robert Mitchum, Teresa Wright).

Colorado Territory (1949; with Joel McCrea, Virginia Mayo).

ADAM'S RIB

Somehow, while you are watching Katharine Hepburn, Spencer Tracy, Judy Holliday, Tom Ewell, and David Wayne in George Cukor's scintillatingly directed 1949 comedy *Adam's Rib*, written brilliantly by Ruth Gordon and Garson Kanin, you feel that by the time it's over the world's millennia-old battle of the sexes will now finally be on the road to ultimate resolution, understanding, peace. And what could be a better feeling on Valentine's Day (February 14)?

Such is the magic of this terrific New York story about two lawyers—one the city prosecutor, the other his wife— and what happens when they get on opposite sides of a headline-grabbing marital case: a wife (Holliday) caught her husband (Ewell) red-handed with his mistress (Jean Hagan) and shot him, not fatally. (This opening sequence is especially memorable and funny.) Tracy is assigned to prosecute, and Hepburn decides to take on the woman's defense, painting her as a wronged female fighting back. Fireworks— public and private—ensue, and by the conclusion, any number of archetypal male-female eruptions have occurred. Both Hepburn and Tracy are remarkably eloquent for their opposing viewpoints, though the picture feels weighted more toward Hepburn's. Very much on her side is their sarcastic Broadway-composer friend (David Wayne), a role inspired by Cole Porter, who himself contributed an original song ("Farewell, Amanda"—Kate's name in the movie). Wayne sings it with all the gusto of a guy who had recently scored a triumph in the original New York production of *Finian's Rainbow*.

Of the nine Tracy-Hepburn vehicles shot during the quarter century between 1942's *Woman of the Year* (directed by George Stevens) and 1967's *Guess Who's Coming to Dinner* (directed by Stanley Kramer), I'd put *Adam's Rib* at the top. The real Manhattan locations certainly help to give it the edge, as does the basic premise—unbeatable in male-female conflict—not to mention Judy Holliday's scene-stealing performance, filmed while she was already wowing Broadway audiences as the lead in Garson Kanin's hit play, *Born Yesterday*.

Columbia Pictures had bought the film rights to *Born Yesterday* and had signed Cukor to direct, with Kanin doing his own screenplay, but studio chief Harry Cohn had already let it be known that he didn't want Judy Holliday to repeat her stage triumph; he didn't consider her screen-star material. So Cukor and Kanin conspired with Hepburn and Tracy to create as meaty a role as possible for Holliday in *Adam's Rib*—produced for MGM—as a kind of screen test extraordinaire for her own *Born Yesterday*. Hepburn made one of the most generous and helpful gestures in Holliday's first extended dialogue scene—a prison interview—by allowing Cukor to let the entire scene play on Holliday. Hepburn is seen only in profile, not so much letting Judy steal it as simply giving it to her. After seeing *Adam's Rib*, Cohn cast Holliday in *Born Yesterday*; a year later she won the Oscar as best actress for it.

Holliday went on to make two more Cukor-Kanin pictures, the final one being Jack Lemmon's first movie, the delightful (though poorly titled by the studio) *It Should Happen to You* (1954). This one is also set in Manhattan and has some memorable Central Park and Columbus Circle segments (see the pre-Coliseum Circle!); it also has great charm, and probably Peter Lawford's best performance.

Cukor, of course, supervised quite a number of Oscar-winning performances from established stars and from newcomers—he discovered Katharine Hepburn (for 1932's *A Bill of Divorcement*). Hepburn and Cukor collaborated on ten pictures (two for TV), and another of their finest featured her incandescent 1933 performance of Louisa May Alcott's Jo in the first and best sound version of *Little Women*. Hard to believe, seeing this four-handkerchief saga of a mother and four daughters growing up in New England in the 1800s, that women then could not vote; or seeing *Adam's Rib*, that women had only had that right for less than thirty years. Now, fifty years after the release of *Adam's Rib*, the true equality of women is *still* an issue. Speaking of equality, the other wonderful Hepburn-Tracy-Cukor-Kanin-Gordon comedy, 1952's *Pat and Mike*, deals with this even more directly, and the two stars' characters agree that for a relationship to really work, it's *got* to be "five-o/five-o."

OTHER GEORGE CUKOR–
KATHARINE HEPBURN–SPENCER TRACY PICTURES:
   Keeper of the Flame (1943; with Angela Lansbury).
   Pat and Mike (1952; with Aldo Ray).

OTHER CUKOR-HEPBURN PICTURES:
   A Bill of Divorcement (1932; with John Barrymore).
   Little Women (1933; with Joan Bennett).
   Love Among the Ruins (1975; with Laurence Olivier; made for TV).
   The Corn Is Green (1979; made for TV).

Also see Week 51.

OTHER CUKOR-TRACY PICTURES:

Edward, My Son (1949; with Deborah Kerr).

The Actress (1953; with Jean Simmons, Anthony Perkins, Teresa Wright).

OTHER CUKOR–JUDY HOLLIDAY PICTURES:

Born Yesterday (1950; with William Holden, Broderick Crawford).

The Marrying Kind (1952; with Aldo Ray).

It Should Happen to You (1954; with Jack Lemmon, Peter Lawford).

OTHER CUKOR COMEDIES:

Dinner at Eight (1933; with Marie Dressler, Jean Harlow, John Barrymore, Lionel Barrymore).

The Women (1939; with Norma Shearer, Joan Crawford, Rosalind Russell).

NOTORIOUS

For an absolutely unique, no-apologies, no-excuses, first-rate picture, Alfred Hitchcock's 1946 suspense success, *Notorious*, is the one. It is a more-modern-than-ever, ambiguous and troubling, love-versus-duty story of the early noir era: a convicted Nazi's innocent daughter (Ingrid Bergman at her most striking), wholly in love with an American spy (Cary Grant) who's divided about her, is forced to marry a renegade Nazi (Claude Rains) who's truly mad about her. Grant once told me: "Yeah, that's the picture Hitch threw to Ingrid. Hitch often threw them to the woman if he could." It is arguably Hitchcock's best film, with a brilliant script (nominated for an Academy Award) that he concocted with the ace Ben Hecht.

His ninth American film—preceded by a decade and a half of fine work in his native England—*Notorious* was to be Hitchcock's third picture for producer David O. Selznick. Their first (and the director's initial U.S. movie) had been *Rebecca*, which won the Oscar as best picture for 1940. He followed this with films more in his style and to his liking, such as *Foreign Correspondent, Suspicion, Saboteur,* and his own personal favorite, *Shadow of a Doubt,* cowritten with Thornton Wilder. After another Selznick-Hitchcock hit, *Spellbound,* which the director didn't like much either, Hitchcock began to conceive of another picture for his

Spellbound star, Ingrid Bergman, whom he adored. But Selznick, for a variety of reasons, did not believe in the essential premise of *Notorious*, and eventually he sold his rights to it, enabling Hitchcock to produce the movie himself. It became Hitchcock's last big success of the Forties and an enduring classic.

It is striking how much the film takes Bergman's side, how thoroughly we come to identify with her character, and all from the way Hitchcock tells the story visually. Among several famous sequences, one of the most memorable is a love scene between Grant and Bergman that starts on the terrace of her Rio apartment and continues, uninterrupted by any cut, into the apartment itself as Cary and Ingrid kiss and hold each other all the way over to the phone.

When I asked Hitchcock about this, he said he got the idea for the shot while observing from his train compartment a young couple walking along a field, holding each other all the while, even as the boy paused to relieve himself by the side of a barn. As Hitch put it: "Love must not be interrupted—even for urination!"

There are numerous typically Hitchcockian touches in *Notorious* (and see Weeks 15 and 32), including the dark ambiguity of Grant's character as well as the inordinate sympathy engendered by Claude Rains's villain. This sympathy arises in part because of a superbly etched performance by Rains (he was Oscar-nominated for best supporting actor), but also because one feels quite palpably through Hitchcock's direction that his love for Bergman is strangely more genuine than Grant's. Only at the very end, when she is nearly dead, does the Grant character come to believe in this woman, who has loved him from the start, done what she's done with such revulsion only for him, to prove her worth. It becomes, therefore, one of Hitchcock's most disturbing love stories, and among his most subtly suspenseful pictures because an inordinate amount of the tension comes not from without but from the psychological pressures and undertones of the characters.

OTHER ALFRED HITCHCOCK–CARY GRANT PICTURES:
Suspicion (1941; with Joan Fontaine).
To Catch a Thief (1955; with Grace Kelly).

Also see Week 32.

OTHER HITCHCOCK–INGRID BERGMAN PICTURES:
Spellbound (1945; with Gregory Peck).
Under Capricorn (1949; with Joseph Cotten).

OTHER HITCHCOCK LOVE STORY/SUSPENSE PICTURES:
Young and Innocent (1937; with Nova Pilbeam, Derrick de Marney).
Rebecca (1940; with Laurence Olivier, Joan Fontaine).
I Confess (1953; with Montgomery Clift, Anne Baxter).
Vertigo (1958; with James Stewart, Kim Novak).
Marnie (1964; with Sean Connery, Tippi Hedren).

John Wayne as Sean Thornton catches Maureen O'Hara as Mary Kate Donaher cleaning up his house for him, and is about to kiss her for the first time in John Ford's comical yet most romantic love story, *The Quiet Man* (Week 11), set in Ireland at its most beautiful. *Photo courtesy Photofest.*

THE BLUE ANGEL

After a late Sixties L.A. university screening of two silent Josef von Sternberg films, I went over to the enigmatic, legendary director and commented to him that both of the female stars in his movies reminded me—in their look and in certain attitudes—of characters later personified in his talkies by Marlene Dietrich, whom Sternberg discovered in Berlin at the end of the Twenties and made into an international star through the seven pictures they did together. Sternberg bristled immediately. "That is ridiculous," he said. "*I* am Miss Dietrich—Miss Dietrich is *me*." Which was actually his own way of confirming what I had been leading up to with my remark—that Dietrich came to embody, in the most perfectly realized, idealized form, certain kinds of women in whom Sternberg had already shown an interest, that in fact he had been extremely influential in creating her extraordinary persona.

A few years later, after Sternberg had died, I met Marlene Dietrich and told her what he had said. She said his words were accurate. "At the studio," she explained, "I just did what he told me, and then I would go home and cook for him." Marlene and Jo lived together for a while, but she broke his heart long before they made their last picture.

Indeed, Sternberg's career never recovered from the initial success (of the first five), and then the dismal failure (of the last two) of his Dietrich pictures. Marlene had a lengthy career; Sternberg's never caught on again. His "creation" long outlived him, but Dietrich always spoke of her Jo with the kind of reverence one generally reserves for God.

In 1930 two radically different Sternberg films did the trick for Dietrich, one in Europe, the other in America. The latter—*Morocco*—was released first in the United States, *before* the former, which was filmed earlier (in Germany) and had made her a sensation on the Continent.

This first Sternberg-Dietrich collaboration was the classic drama of passion and betrayal, *The Blue Angel.* It was shot simultaneously in German and English—a not unusual custom in the early sound era. The English-language version was lost for years, and more recent generations (like mine) have seen only the subtitled version, which is universally considered better because the cast of German actors were naturally more comfortable in their mother tongue.

The top-billed star of *Der Blaue Engel*, after all, was that most distinguished of German actors Emil Jannings, who had been the first ever to win an Oscar for best actor—for Sternberg's silent masterwork *The Last Command* (1928). Jannings was so happy with this American picture that he specifically asked for Sternberg to come to Germany to direct the star's first talking film: another of Jannings's typical riches-to-rags downfall dramas begun brilliantly with Ernst Lubitsch in the late teens, and reaching extraordinary heights with F. W. Murnau's watershed film, *The Last Laugh* (1925). Little did Jannings know that his unknown costar, his ultrasexy nemesis in *The Blue Angel*, would shortly supersede him in stardom and popularity, or that the film would be his last American success. With Hitler's ascendance, Jannings remained in Nazi Germany, where he was honored. But when the war was over, so was Jannings, whose end was as ignominious in life as it usually was on the screen.

But *The Blue Angel* instantly set Dietrich among the immortals, and her chair-straddling portrayal of cabaret singer Lola-Lola defined her essential image in certain irrevocable ways. She would forever sing the song she is doing the first time we see her: "Falling in love again/. . . Never wanted to/ What am I to do?/Can't help it." In other words, she too was a fool for love, like all the men who fell for her.

Talking with Sternberg another time, I said that *The Blue Angel* was actually the only time Dietrich really destroyed a man, to which he replied: "She did not destroy him—he destroyed himself. It was his mistake—he should never have taken up with her. That's what the story is."

Jannings is a prudish boys'-school teacher who falls madly in love with the loose and bawdy cabaret singer, who can't possibly be faithful. The strain breaks him down to ultimate degradation, as in that line from Jacques Brel's masochistic love chant, *"Ne me quitte pas"*: Jannings becomes nearly content to be to Dietrich "the shadow of your dog." The moment when Marlene humiliates Jannings by making him crow like a rooster for her is one of the most chilling in picture history. It was a scene Sternberg added. The amazing chiaroscuro photography, the clothing, the decor, the atmosphere: with Dietrich at her least sentimental, Jannings at his most naked, everything conspires to make *The Blue Angel* an indelible screen tragedy.

OTHER JOSEF VON STERNBERG–MARLENE DIETRICH PICTURES:
Morocco (1930; with Gary Cooper, Adolph Menjou).
Dishonored (1931; with Victor McLaglen).
Shanghai Express (1932; with Clive Brook).
Blonde Venus (1932; with Cary Grant, Herbert Marshall).

The Scarlet Empress (1934; with John Lodge, Sam Jaffe).
The Devil Is a Woman (1935; with Cesar Romero).

ANOTHER STERNBERG–EMIL JANNINGS PICTURE:
The Last Command (1928; with Evelyn Brent, William Powell).

OTHER STERNBERG PICTURES:
The Salvation Hunters (1925; with Georgia Hale).
Underworld (1927; with George Bancroft).
The Docks of New York (1928; with George Bancroft).
The Shanghai Gesture (1941; with Gene Tierney).
The Saga of Anatahan (1953; narrated by Sternberg).

THE MIRACLE OF MORGAN'S CREEK

I simply couldn't believe my eyes the first time I saw Preston Sturges's outrageous, subversive 1944 slapstick romantic comedy, *The Miracle of Morgan's Creek.* What got me was the (still) amazingly fresh combination of utterly sophisticated plot and viewpoint—Sturges had an eccentric and artistic mother and was raised in Europe—with flat-out falling-down American farce.

Of course, Sturges wrote and directed at least seven of the best talking comedies ever made in America, and he made those seven (plus a studio-truncated drama) all within the same four-year period, 1940–1944: a burst of creativity like no other in picture history (see Weeks 2 and 40).

But that Sturges could, in the midst of the censorship-dominated war years, get away with this story line is by itself a marvel: young woman lies to her father, sneaks off to a soldiers' farewell party, gets so drunk that all she can remember the morning after is impulsively "marrying" some G.I. whose name she can't even recall; soon, however, she finds herself pregnant in her small hometown with no provable husband . . . Yes, the infamous Production Code, which spelled out what you couldn't do, was tough—but not if you really had talent! Restrictions or limitations can be rewarding challenges to inventive and resourceful artists.

Sturges seems to have thrived on such obstacles throughout his heyday.

Of course, Sturges had at least three absolutely brilliant comic actors—Eddie Bracken (at his very best here and in Sturges's other superb 1944 film, *Hail the Conquering Hero*), William Demarest (featured in many other Sturges pictures, but at his wildest in this; he does several amazing pratfalls here that take the cake), Betty Hutton (her top performance)—plus the usual terrific character actors from this writer-director's famous stock company. Sturges even has the moxie to reprise two of the characters from his own first film, *The Great McGinty* (1940), with Brian Donlevy and Akim Tamiroff playing Morgan's Creek's state governor and his mob-boss. Sturges usually wrote for actors he intended to cast, using some of their peculiarities and personalities to help erase the line between actor and character. Originally a key element in moviemaking, this close fit is unfortunately often lost today because of most actors' (understandable) desire to prove range and versatility.

Not only are all the performances top-notch but there's that flawless comic rhythm that is uniquely Sturges—his stock company certainly knew his beat—like a conductor with his own orchestra. This was especially important with Sturges, who created all his scripts by improvising them for his secretary to write down. His widow, Sandy Sturges, who served as his girl Friday for a while, told me he was one really hilarious performer.

There are a couple of lines in the movie—"The spots!" and "Ignatz Ratzkeywatzkey"—that have become catchphrases in our family, as they might in yours if the wavelength Sturges is operating on connects. For peak watchability, this movie deserves an audience; so invite as many laughers as possible to see one of the funniest talking pictures ever made.

ANOTHER PRESTON STURGES–EDDIE BRACKEN PICTURE:
  Hail the Conquering Hero (1944; with William Demarest, Ella Raines).

OTHER STURGES COMEDIES:
  Mad Wednesday (a.k.a. *The Sin of Harold Diddlebock*; 1947; with Harold Lloyd, Frances Ramsden).
  Unfaithfully Yours (1948; with Rex Harrison, Linda Darnell, Rudy Vallee).

Also see Weeks 2 and 40.

THE QUIET MAN

For decades, when I would tell certain killjoys that one of my all-time favorite films is John Ford's robust, luminously Technicolored 1952 Irish love story–comedy, *The Quiet Man,* they would say condescendingly, "You know, the Irish aren't really like that." Well, a couple of years ago, I finally got a chance to go to Ireland and found to my delight that actually the Irish are a good deal "like that." And Ireland itself is even more gloriously beautiful than it looks in Ford's movie, which stars John Wayne at his most leading-man likable and Maureen O'Hara at her most gorgeously feisty. (For St. Patrick's Day—March 17—there could hardly be another choice.)

The Quiet Man was a homecoming story Ford had wanted to do since the mid-1930s, and only after he had agreed to make his third cavalry-and-Indians film *(Rio Grande),* did mini-major Republic Studios allow him to make the movie, which became perhaps his biggest commercial success and for which he received his fourth Oscar as best director (still the record).

Wayne plays a popular Irish-American prizefighter who has accidentally killed an opponent in the ring and sworn off fighting, and who returns to his long-unseen homeland, buys the cottage of his long-lost mother's dreams, and falls in love at first sight with his neighbor's sister (O'Hara). The hitch is that her brother (splendidly done by Victor McLaglen) is a mean-spirited bully who coveted the land Wayne bought, takes out his disappointments on his sister's relationship, and refuses to provide her dowry. As a result, O'Hara, feeling she is still not her own woman, refuses Wayne the privileges of the wedding night, or any conjugal night, until she receives her furniture and personal belongings.

The essential simplicity of the plot belies the delightful though deeply felt complexities of the telling. There is no other film in Ford's canon like it, yet the work seems nearly the most personal he ever made, done with a lightness of touch that perfectly combines charm with an inherent gravity. Having spent nearly five years of his life in World War II and having lost the love of his life (Katharine Hepburn) because of duty and tradition, Ford here reveals his most heartfelt emotions without pretension or pomposity. Ford was fifty-seven when he made the movie, and it has romantic abandon checked by wisdom, a sense of whimsy combined with rueful knowledge. It is no coincidence that O'Hara's character-name is Mary Kate—Mary after Ford's long-suffering wife, mother of his two children; Kate after Hepburn, the love that was reciprocal but couldn't be. I remember once being with Ford, less than two years before he died, when he was told he had a phone call from Hepburn, and I can never forget the boyish and happy way he said, "Kate?!" as he went to answer it.

The Quiet Man, while it endorses pacifism, a need for peace—which Ford undoubtedly yearned for and never achieved—nonetheless speaks strongly of the absolute necessity to fight for a just cause, and of the belief that a man must willingly undergo the ordeals of Hercules to win a woman's love. Finally, the picture is a fable of wish fulfillment, a vision of life not as it necessarily is, but as it should be: where Catholic and Protestant join together to fight for love; where there is equal respect for both sexes, though they may have different roles, albeit ones that may overlap; where chivalry, honor, and gallantry are not words in the punch line of a dirty joke.

No words, however, can convey the joyous exuberance of *The Quiet Man*, its visual grace, the wonderful love of humanity it projects. Barry Fitzgerald's performance alone as "the matchmaker" carries much of the leprechaunlike magic and poetic mystery Ford brings to the tale. It is, too, a film for the whole family, before ratings were necessary, that is thoroughly clear for adults in its adult meanings, yet innocently enjoyable for children.

On its highest level, the mythological one, *The Quiet Man* is a comic variation on the single most ancient mythic tale, that of the queen or goddess and the two sacred kings or gods who fight and kill each other yearly for her affections. Unquestionably Ford had read an old Irish version of the Cuchulain saga in which the Holly Knight (Wayne) spares the Oak Knight (McLaglen) for the sake of the queen (O'Hara). Jack Ford knew his Celtic mythology and all about those ancient Druids. He was extremely well read, especially in history and prehistory (there always being several stacks of arcane books of that sort on his night tables both at home and on location). And he, more consciously perhaps than any other of the pioneer picture-makers, knew that he was working in a much larger than life and therefore mythically potent medium. (Remember, this was before reduction-to-video size.) It is also no coincidence that John Wayne remains one of America's favorite and most enduring stars even some two decades after his death: John Ford used Wayne (about twenty times) as the ultimate American sacred king, and he knew what he was doing; he always used to say, "Heroes are good for the country."

OTHER JOHN FORD–JOHN WAYNE–MAUREEN O'HARA PICTURES:
  Rio Grande (1950; with Ben Johnson, Harry Carey Jr.).
  The Wings of Eagles (1957; with Dan Dailey).

ANOTHER FORD-WAYNE COMEDY:
  Donovan's Reef (1963; with Lee Marvin, Elizabeth Allen, Dorothy Lamour).

OTHER FORD LOVE STORIES/COMEDIES:
  The Whole Town's Talking (1935; with Edward G. Robinson, Jean Arthur).
  Steamboat 'Round the Bend (1935; with Will Rogers).
  When Willie Comes Marching Home (1950; with Dan Dailey).

Also see Weeks 22, 38, and 50.

HEAVEN CAN WAIT

Several of my all-time favorite films were directed by the same filmmaker—the inimitable though much imitated Ernst Lubitsch. A popular and innovative genius, to be remembered especially for the irresistible sparkle of his comedies and musicals (and what could be better for the start of spring?), Lubitsch was a Berliner of Polish and German-Jewish extraction who, as Jean Renoir said to me in the Sixties, "invented the modern Hollywood." By "modern," Renoir meant Hollywood films from about 1925 through the late 1940s—when Lubitsch died—and even into the next two decades.

In his day, Lubitsch was probably the most respected among his peers, and his name was a household word. Everybody had heard that universal phrase of praise the "Lubitsch Touch," which was a way of describing his often oblique storytelling, a certain style that was unmistakable yet difficult to describe. Today, except among true film aficionados and scholars, Lubitsch is barely talked about. Yet Billy Wilder, perhaps the last survivor from the golden age of movies, always used to have a sign on the wall of his screenwriting rooms: HOW WOULD LUBITSCH HAVE DONE IT?

One of the master's most wonderful and representative films, one that should be seen by anybody who craves real quality or needs to be convinced that there has been a general dumbing down of our popular entertainment, is Lubitsch's penultimate film. Appropriately, the 1943 Technicolor production *Heaven Can Wait* is a look at the inevitability of death and a meditation on the rewards and punishments of the afterlife, all part of a funny and profoundly human chronicle of an unimportant man's life.

The famous Lubitsch style was achieved in part by the director's practice of acting out all the roles for all the actors, from the bit players to the stars. Lubitsch was a not-very-tall, heavyset man with a thick German accent, but he had begun in silent pictures as a star comedian and his sense of timing was impeccable.

Jack Benny had been in Lubitsch's darkest comedy, *To Be or Not to Be* (1942), and I asked him once how the director's acting-out had been. "Well," Jack said, "it was a little *broad*, but you got the idea!" And so in *Heaven Can Wait*, Don Ameche gives the performance of his career and Gene Tierney is at her spunkiest yet most beautifully vulnerable.

The intricately constructed screenplay—the story told in flashback as Ameche comes to the entrance of Hell and must explain his life—was written with Lubitsch by his longtime collaborator and friend, playwright Samson Raphaelson. I once lunched with Raphaelson, and he told me how Ameche had come to be cast, despite the fact that Ameche was neither Lubitsch's nor Raphaelson's first choice. Lubitsch had phoned Raphaelson and said in his heavy accent, "Sam, we got a problem." What was it? Lubitsch told him that 20th Century-Fox studio head Darryl Zanuck would do anything for Lubitsch but had now asked the director to do him a favor and make a test of Ameche, Fox's top male star. Lubitsch hastened to tell Raphaelson that obviously they didn't have to use the actor—neither admired him much—but that he couldn't refuse Zanuck the screen test. Raphaelson agreed, so long as they didn't have to cast Ameche. A week or so later,

Raphaelson went on, Lubitsch called again and said, "Sam, we got a problem. Can you come down to the studio—I want to show you something." So Raphaelson went, and Lubitsch ran Ameche's test for him. When it was over, Raphaelson, surprised, exclaimed: "He's good!" "Yah," Lubitsch said ruefully, "that's our problem. . . ."

Indeed, Ameche is *echt* Lubitsch in the leading role. In support, Marjorie Main, Eugene Pallette, Louis Calhern, Signe Hasso, and Laird Cregar are all terrific in the director's most forgiving farewell to "the good life."

OTHER ERNST LUBITSCH COMEDIES:
> *Trouble in Paradise* (1932; with Herbert Marshall, Miriam Hopkins, Kay Francis).
> *Ninotchka* (1939; with Greta Garbo, Melvyn Douglas).
> *To Be or Not to Be* (1942; with Carole Lombard, Jack Benny, Robert Stack).
> *Cluny Brown* (1946; with Charles Boyer, Jennifer Jones).

Also see Weeks 49 and 52.

THE KID

A quintessential work in American film history—written, produced, directed by, and starring an Englishman—*The Kid* is Charlie Chaplin's classic 1921 comedy, the first feature-length work (after scores of shorts) to star his indelible creation, the Tramp. (A good way to celebrate April Fools' Day.) I was weaned on *The Kid*, seeing it first at New York's Museum of Modern Art in the mid-1940s when the picture was barely twenty-five years old. Seventy-eight years after its release, this testament to Chaplin's unique genius with pathos comedy still retains its magic glow, as the Tramp tries to bring up a six-year-old orphan, in an exhilaratingly fresh performance from newcomer Jackie Coogan carefully coached, maneuvered, and manipulated by Chaplin.

Remember, Charlie Chaplin was, at the time of this movie's initial release, the most popular and deeply beloved human being on earth, maybe in the history of the world. In its own day, *The Kid* was the second biggest grossing movie ever released, right after D. W. Griffith's 1915 landmark, *The Birth of a Nation*. You can still see why: the potent mixture of irreverent slapstick comedy with a kind of Dickensian squalor and sense of tragedy remains unbeatable. (The 1998 Italian film *Life Is Beautiful* is a recent version.)

Told once that his camera angles were not at all interesting, Chaplin responded: "They don't have to be—*I* am interesting." That was putting it mildly. Beginning with the two-reelers he wrote, directed, and starred in from about 1915 to 1917, Chaplin soon became the most popular performer in the movies. His success continued with his three- and four-reel comedies of 1918–1923. After *The Kid*, which was probably the best of his work to that point, the features continued his glory, but at ever-longer intervals— with only *The Gold Rush* (1925) and *The Circus* (1928) left as Tramp features in the silent period. Indeed, the pure Tramp appeared only twice in the sound era, and both of these features—*City Lights* (1931) and *Modern Times* (1936)—are essentially nontalking films with music and effects. (In the latter, Chaplin does sing one song in pseudo-French gibberish.)

At the end of *Modern Times*, when Chaplin and nineteen-year-old Paulette Goddard (who had secretly become his third wife during shooting) walked off into the sunset down the never-ending highway, it was the Tramp's final appearance and the end of an era Chaplin had dominated for two decades. His popularity never regained this level, but slipped progressively throughout the 1940s until his departure from the United States in 1952. Told by the State Department that because of moral and political reasons—he was a suspected Communist and had just taken as his fourth bride the eighteen-year-old Oona O'Neill—he would not be admitted back into the country that had made him rich, but of which he had never become a citizen, Chaplin vowed never to return.

Twenty years later, he did come back, to receive his second Special Oscar. For that 1972 tribute, I had been asked to prepare the montage of Chaplin clips that would precede his entrance. Of the thirteen and a half minutes I chose, the final four and a half were from the last sequence of *The Kid*. As Charlie ran to save Jackie and took him back into his arms for the fade-out, there wasn't a dry eye in the house. Coogan was there that night, too, and afterward, at the Academy ball, Chaplin commented to me on the montage. Looking bewildered, tears in his eyes, he said: "Jackie Coogan . . . Jackie Coogan . . . he was a tiny little boy . . . and now he's an old fat man."

But on the screen, Jackie and Charlie will be forever young, forever wonderfully larcenous as they brave the cruel world. In his own grim childhood, Chaplin had himself been a poverty-stricken kid—his father dead, his mother driven insane—dancing and clowning on London streets with his half-brother for a few shillings. These Dickensian beginnings are nowhere more sharply drawn than in *The Kid*, one of the crowning glories of the silent era, and Chaplin's first mature masterwork of comedy-tragedy.

OTHER CHARLIE CHAPLIN COMEDIES:
The Floorwalker (1916; short).
The Fireman (1916; short).
The Vagabond (1916; short).
The Count (1916; short).
The Pawnshop (1916; short).
Easy Street (1917; short).
The Cure (1917; short).
The Immigrant (1917; short).
A Dog's Life (1918; featurette).
Shoulder Arms (1918; featurette).
The Pilgrim (1923; featurette).
The Gold Rush (1925; with Georgia Hale, Mack Swain).
The Circus (1928; with Merna Kennedy).
City Lights (1931; with Virginia Cherrill).
Modern Times (1936; with Paulette Goddard).

Ginger Rogers is supposedly teaching Fred Astaire how to dance, and she is both delighted and smitten to find that he seems to be pretty good at it in their first number ("Pick Yourself Up") from George Stevens's *Swing Time* (Week 17), with music by Jerome Kern.

Photo courtesy Photofest.

OUT OF THE PAST

The most strangely poetic of crime thrillers (known chicly these days as films noir), Jacques Tourneur's memorable 1947 romantic suspense classic *Out of the Past*, is also one of the great movie titles and features Robert Mitchum's first (and probably most) defining role for his screen persona. Mitchum plays a former detective now working in a small-town garage, in the hope that his past won't catch up with him. But it always does, especially the past you're trying so hard to forget: in this case, the vulnerable, lovely, and very dangerous woman he fell for, acted enticingly by Jane Greer, and the smooth, lethal gangster she comes attached to, played to perfection by a young Kirk Douglas (in only his fourth film).

The superbly constructed screenplay—with an extended flashback beautifully narrated by Mitchum—was done by Daniel Mainwaring, under his crime-author pseudonym Geoffrey Homes, and based on his own novel *Build My Gallows High*—the picture's title in Britain. (The story was remade, after a fashion, in 1984 as *Against All Odds*, starring Jeff Bridges.) The black-and-white photography by Nicholas Musuraca, much of it shot on real locations, is especially evocative, but the overall quality of passionate understatement, of a certain sadly clear-eyed empathy for all the doomed characters, comes from Jacques Tourneur.

This feeling can be found in all Tourneur's finest work, even with the most unlikely material, from a subtle horror picture like *Cat People* (1942) to a low-keyed Joel McCrea Western like *Stars in My Crown* (1950). It is the Frenchman in him.

Born in Paris, Tourneur grew up with the movies. His father, pioneer director-producer Maurice Tourneur—a student of sculptor Auguste Rodin—was (particularly during the silent era) one of the giants of the French and the American screen, and was most distinguished by his work on mystery-horror-fantasy films. The master himself, Alfred Hitchcock, told me that among the pictures which most impressed him as a youth was Maurice Tourneur's fantastic *The Isle of Lost Ships* (1923).

As a youngster, Jacques first worked on his father's pictures, soon was off on his own and, being a good son, did not want to figuratively kill the father, so never seems to have aspired to the kind of size and popularity the elder Tourneur's work achieved. Instead, Jacques went the other way. His more modest accomplishments, however, have an equally enduring value, with many film buffs singling out not only his civilized horror pictures, but his consistently human series of Joel McCrea Westerns. Although *Out of the Past* is his best film, there's overall a literate, modest charm to Tourneur's work, which gives the impression that he was a particularly amiable person.

OTHER JACQUES TOURNEUR PICTURES:
   Cat People (1942; with Simone Simon, Kent Smith).
   I Walked with a Zombie (1943; with Frances Dee, Tom Conway).
   The Leopard Man (1943; with Dennis O'Keefe, Isabel Jewell).
   Days of Glory (1944; with Gregory Peck).

Experiment Perilous (1944; with Hedy Lamarr, George Brent).

Canyon Passage (1946; with Dana Andrews, Susan Hayward).

Berlin Express (1948; with Robert Ryan, Merle Oberon).

The Flame and the Arrow (1950; with Burt Lancaster).

Stars in My Crown (1950; with Joel McCrea).

Appointment in Honduras (1953; with Glenn Ford, Ann Sheridan).

Stranger on Horseback (1955; with Joel McCrea).

Wichita (1955; with Joel McCrea).

Great Day in the Morning (1956; with Robert Stack, Ruth Roman, Virginia Mayo).

Curse of the Demon (1957; with Dana Andrews).

The Comedy of Terrors (1963; with Vincent Price, Boris Karloff, Peter Lorre).

STRANGERS ON A TRAIN

In the 1950s, the conventional critical wisdom about Alfred Hitchcock was that his best work was done in England in the Thirties. In truth, much of his best work was done in America in the Fifties. That was the decade of such extremely personal, if not especially successful, pictures as *I Confess* (1953) and *Vertigo* (1958), as well as such popular vintage achievements as *Rear Window* (1954), *To Catch a Thief* (1955), and *North by Northwest* (1959).

The movie that kicked off this amazing cycle, though a substantial hit in its time and certainly among his finest, is for some reason rarely cited as such these days: 1951's rivetingly suspenseful *Strangers on a Train*, adapted from Patricia Highsmith's novel. Maybe this is because it's in black and white and boasts no enduring superstar like Cary Grant or James Stewart. Nevertheless, it remains among his most fully realized and unsettling thrillers, with at least three memorably effective sequences and featuring one of the most brilliantly subversive performances in any Hitchcock movie.

Prior to *Strangers*, Robert Walker had been almost as much identified as the all-American boy next door as Anthony Perkins had before Hitch cast him in *Psycho* (1960). Walker was an especially personable actor—his most defining role being the young soldier who falls for Judy Garland

STRANGERS ON A TRAIN 65

in Vincente Minnelli's lovely wartime fable, *The Clock* (1944)—and Hitchcock here used his indisputable likability and charm to a superbly perverse effect. Indeed, it's Walker's charismatic persona, as much as Hitchcock's camera work and cutting, that makes the central plot device work so well. Two strangers meet by chance on a train, have a couple of drinks, talk about their lives; one (a tennis star played by Farley Granger) is very unhappily married, the other (a spoiled mama's-boy neurotic) loathes his father and half-jokingly (or is he joking at all?) proposes they swap murders: Walker's character will kill the wife if Granger's will kill the father. Since they cannot be linked to each other, there is no motive and the murders can never be solved.

The opening sequence is among Hitchcock's most masterfully done: cross-cutting only between two different pairs of shoes, the director follows each from taxi to train station to train, not revealing who the characters are until, in the lounge car, one's shoe accidentally bumps the other's. Then comes the long, complex duologue which, when Hitchcock described it to his first scenarist on the film, Raymond Chandler (legendary creator of detective Philip Marlowe), completely bewildered him. Chandler felt there was simply no way to impart all the nuances Hitchcock wanted: a joking/not joking proposal, totally unaccepted by one, yet believed to be agreed to by the other, none of it spelled out, all by inference. But Chandler was thinking of the printed word while Hitchcock was seeing it on the screen, where choice of angle, size of image, timing of cuts, and the intonations and personalities of the actors all play a role in achieving effects. Upon seeing the finished movie, Chandler had to admit Hitchcock had accomplished everything he had described.

Equally remarkable, in more obviously gripping ways,

are the murder at a carnival of the rather sluttish wife (an exceptional performance by Laura Elliott)—the actual strangulation seen only as reflected in the lenses of the victim's fallen eyeglasses—and the final extended fight between Walker and Granger on an out-of-control merry-go-round, kids and parents screaming as the thing whirls wildly. The daunting complexities of shooting this sequence never get in the way of Hitchcock's flawless manipulation.

Probably the most Hitchockian aspect of *Strangers on a Train* is the chilling ambiguity of the situation—the transference of guilt, a theme the director often explored. After all, Walker's cold-blooded murder—again made possible and believable through the use of the actor's intrinsic charm in luring the woman to her doom—does actually free Granger from the terrible dilemma he was in, making it possible for him to marry the rich girl he really loves (a nice job by Ruth Roman). Hitchcock keeps this terrible irony clearly present to the end.

While this was just the beginning of an extraordinary decade for the Master of Suspense, the picture would be the last one Robert Walker completed before his tragic death from a heart attack at age thirty-three the same year as its release. The troubled, gifted actor—he had had drinking problems and a mental breakdown—was filming Leo McCarey's *My Son John* (1952), and McCarey had to borrow some of Hitchcock's footage to finish his movie.

OTHER ALFRED HITCHCOCK THRILLERS:
   The Man Who Knew Too Much (1934; with Leslie Banks, Edna Best, Peter Lorre).
   The Lady Vanishes (1938; with Michael Redgrave).
   Shadow of a Doubt (1943; with Joseph Cotten, Teresa Wright).
   Dial M for Murder (1954; with Ray Milland, Grace Kelly, Robert Cummings).

The Man Who Knew Too Much (1956; with James Stewart, Doris Day).
Psycho (1960; with Anthony Perkins, Janet Leigh).
Frenzy (1972; with Jon Finch, Alec McCowen).

Also see Weeks 8 and 32.

GRAND ILLUSION

In any authoritative list of the ten best films ever made, right at the top, or within the top five, is Jean Renoir's unforgettable World War I prisoner-of-war drama from 1937, *Grand Illusion (La Grande Illusion)*. Renoir—youngest son of the great French Impressionist painter Auguste Renoir—was Orson Welles's favorite director, and Welles used to say that if he could take only one movie to the proverbial desert isle, it would be *Grand Illusion*. The first foreign film ever nominated for the Academy's best picture award (played in French and in German, though certain key scenes are spoken in English), the work has extraordinary scope in its human dimensions and the most wide-ranging of historical reverberations—poignantly illuminating, among other things, the conclusive end of aristocracy.

Four archetypes of the period are superbly evoked through transfixing performances from the most durable of French superstars, Jean Gabin (working-class man of the people); from splendid character actor Marcel Dalio (Jewish upper middle class); from elegant French star Pierre Fresnay (French aristocracy); and from the legendary picture-maker and star Erich von Stroheim (German aristocracy). For Renoir, the picture was especially personal, since he had served with the French army—Gabin wears his uniform in the movie—and was wounded three times, almost losing a leg, and walking with a limp for the rest of his life. Personal, too, was the casting of Stroheim, whose strikingly realistic silent films had been an early influence on, and inspiration to, Renoir.

For Americans entering the Great War, as well as for so many others, this was "the war to end all wars"; as the world would see less than two years after the release of this picture, *that* was "the grand illusion." Renoir and his cowriter, the distinguished Charles Spaak, saw the conflict coming and hoped that by dramatizing the essential commonality of the French and German aristocracy they might help to prevent an all-out war. There has never been a more powerful anti-war, prohumanity picture, but artistry, poetry, and the film's worldwide popularity didn't have the smallest effect on Hitler's grander plans.

The plot is simple: A group of captured French officers are held as prisoners in a distant German camp, and a few plan their escape, which only two achieve.

Although Renoir had already been working in films for twelve years, *Grand Illusion* was his first international success, and it remains his most famous work. From the start of the sound era, he had experimented with deep-focus photography—keeping everything sharp in the frame—and with the moving camera, both ways of sustaining actors' performances without the need to cut. These techniques were to have a profound influence on directors the world over, especially in the early work of Orson Welles (see Weeks 18, 26, and 39). Renoir's earliest success was the delightful, quietly antiestablishment 1932 comedy *Boudu Saved from Drowning* (remade in the United States as *Down and Out in Beverly Hills*). His 1935 *Toni*, shot on real streets with nonactors, predated by over a decade the similarly intentioned Italian neorealist movement (see Week 31). In 1936, a further superb development of his moving camera technique came with *The Crime of Mr. Lange* (see Week 37). But *Grand Illusion* spoke to people the world over in a way that no other French film ever had before. With beautiful black-and-white photography by Christian Mathas, and a haunting score by Joseph Kosma, the picture has a deceptive simplicity and carries a richly poetic subtext that helps to make it deeply memorable.

Whenever I want to remind myself that the movies are indeed capable of accomplishments on a level with a Turner painting or a Mozart symphony, I run a Renoir film, especially *The Rules of the Game* (see Week 48) or *Grand Illusion*. The French New Wave filmmakers considered Renoir the greatest of Western directors and were profoundly inspired by his humanist viewpoint and eternal freshness. Certainly there has never been a better picture-maker, and *Grand Illusion* is one of the screen's few truly indispensable works. Seeing it at least once a year is a good idea.

OTHER JEAN RENOIR–JEAN GABIN PICTURES:
   The Lower Depths (1936; with Louis Jouvet).
   La Bête Humaine (1938; with Simone Simon).
   French Cancan (1955; with Françoise Arnoul).

OTHER RENOIR WAR PICTURES:
   La Marseillaise (1938; with Pierre Renoir, Louis Jouvet).
   This Land Is Mine (1943; with Charles Laughton, Maureen O'Hara).
   The Elusive Corporal (1962; with Jean-Pierre Cassel, Claude Brasseur).

Also see Weeks 37 and 48.

"Waitin' 'round the bend, my Huckleberry friend . . . Moon River," sings the immortal Audrey Hepburn as Holly Golightly in Blake Edwards's affecting comedy-drama based on the Truman Capote short novel, *Breakfast at Tiffany's* (Week 19); music by Henry Mancini; lyrics by Johnny Mercer; script by George Axelrod.
Photo courtesy Photofest.

SWING TIME

Talk about the subtle (and often not-so-subtle) effect of a director's personality on his material! When George Stevens was assigned to do a Fred Astaire–Ginger Rogers vehicle at RKO Radio Pictures in 1936, he had come off of doing light (or silly) comedies at that same studio, having begun as cameraman and then director for some of the Stan Laurel–Oliver Hardy two-reelers of the late 1920s and early 1930s. He had also directed, in the previous year, two highly successful vehicles: one for Katharine Hepburn *(Alice Adams)*, the other for Barbara Stanwyck *(Annie Oakley)*.

Stevens's eighth feature and only his third A-picture was the sixth time (out of eleven times) that Astaire and Rogers appeared in a picture together, and it remains the best (if not originally the most popular) of the lot—*Swing Time*. (A good way for lovers to spend May Eve or May Day.) The director scored a theatrical coup by noticing the similarity (from certain angles) between Stan Laurel and Fred Astaire, and for the first twenty minutes of *Swing Time*, the absurd plot and Stevens's shrewd camera placement put Fred Astaire into a Stan Laurel posture. Which plays perfectly into the picture's single most delightful aspect: the witty, clever, and ultimately exhilarating way in which Astaire and Rogers come to dance together for the first time in the story.

First, there's a cute meet out on the street, with a cop and plenty of misunderstanding, so Fred follows Ginger to where she works as—what else?—a ballroom dance instructor. More complications and delays as Fred pretends to be hopelessly incompetent as a dancer; this, plus the previous business on the street, puts Ginger in a mood and her wisecracks get her fired. To coax her job back for her, Fred has to prove to the boss how much she has taught him and now, finally, he sheds Stan Laurel to become—presto—Fred Astaire: only the greatest screen dancer of his time! Big close-up of Ginger as she recognizes her soul mate, and off they dance for an unbroken few minutes of sheer delight, like a mainliner of pure joy. The song they dance to—which had to have had great inspirational value to Depression audiences on its initial release—couldn't exactly hurt us these days either: "Pick Yourself Up (dust yourself off, start all over again)."

This is only the first of the delectable dances Astaire and Rogers do with six Jerome Kern tunes in *Swing Time*, usually in one- or two-camera setups only—for all those in search of an antidote to MTV's cut-cut-cut heritage on TV and on the big screen. So pleasant to see something in real time, without manipulation: photographic magic, lightning captured.

The 1936 Oscar for best song went to the key ballad here, that instant standard "The Way You Look Tonight," which Astaire introduces in his usual smooth, simple way. Another highpoint is the "Never Gonna Dance" finale, and the amazing tribute Astaire pays to legendary black dancer Bill "Bojangles" Robinson—the only time Fred ever did anything of this sort, going into blackface for it, with the number being nominated by the Academy for best dance direction. When I once visited with Astaire, in answer to my question about who his greatest influence had been as a dancer, he replied without hesitation that it was Bill Robinson. "The way he moved . . . !" Astaire said as he got up to show me the elegance he was describing, and of course, with the least effort seemed himself to float across the room.

The sweet heartbreak of Kern's music; the cleverness of Dorothy Fields's lyrics; the charm of the second bananas, Victor Moore and Helen Broderick—not to mention the ever-welcome Eric Blore; and the better-than-average script by Howard Lindsay and Allen Scott—all these conspire to make *Swing Time* a truly enduring entertainment. Director Stanley Donen, who's had a hand in some musical landmarks himself, said to me that *all* the Astaire-Rogers musical numbers in *all* the films were "pure honey"—and, in our home-video era, eminently fast-forwardable to. But two of their movies are worth watching all the way through: *Swing Time* and that 1935 Irving Berlin–Mark Sandrich "Cheek to Cheek" winner, with the most archetypal title of all, *Top Hat.*

ANOTHER GEORGE STEVENS–FRED ASTAIRE PICTURE:
   A Damsel in Distress (1937; with Joan Fontaine, George Burns, Gracie Allen).

ANOTHER STEVENS–GINGER ROGERS PICTURE:
   Vivacious Lady (1938; with James Stewart, Charles Coburn).

OTHER STEVENS COMEDIES:
   Alice Adams (1935; with Katharine Hepburn, Fred MacMurray).
   Woman of the Year (1942; with Spencer Tracy, Katharine Hepburn).
   The More the Merrier (1943; with Jean Arthur, Joel McCrea, Charles Coburn).

CITIZEN KANE

One Manhattan night in 1969, Orson Welles and I had dinner at Frankie and Johnnie's Restaurant with Norman Mailer, whom Welles had just met on a talk show. As soon as we sat down, Mailer asked about a particularly memorable shot in Orson's famous and infamous first film, that still amazing 1941 explosion of genius, *Citizen Kane*. Orson groaned slightly, saying, "Oh, Norman, not *Citizen Kane* . . ." Mailer looked surprised for a moment and then, with a tiny smile of recognition, connected this to his own first novel: "Mmm, yeah—it's like me and *The Naked and the Dead*." Orson nodded, laughing loudly— two American artists acknowledging the terrible stigmatic burden of early success.

The celebrated Broadway entrepreneur Billy Rose had immediately recognized this with Welles; right after seeing *Kane* he had told Welles, who had been an unbelievable twenty-five when he directed, produced, cowrote, and starred in the movie: "Quit, kid—you'll never top it." Indeed, throughout the rest of his life, Welles would read or hear that tired old question: "What did he ever do after *Citizen Kane*?"

The painful irony here is that although *Kane* initially received nearly unanimous critical praise, the film was blacklisted by the Hearst Corporation newspaper chain because it was partially based on certain events in press lord William Randolph Hearst's life. The movie received poor distribution therefore and was by no means a financial winner. It really wasn't until the late Fifties and early Sixties that the picture began to gather the kind of immortal legend of priceless quality it now carries, internationally acknowledged as either the best film ever made, or certainly high among the ten best of all time.

Generally, the work was used as a truncheon to beat up Welles, even after many simultaneous attempts to take as much credit as possible away from him: "Photographic marvel Gregg Toland really did all those striking compositions," "Old-time screenwriter Herman J. Mankiewicz really wrote it," and numerous other mistaken, envious efforts to reduce the monumental weight of Welles's achievement. All right then, who acted the title role? Perhaps this was all some trick of mirrors, too, and it isn't really Welles giving one of the most astoundingly complex and layered performances—from youth to old age—ever captured on film. An awful aspect of human nature: how true greatness seems to humiliate and threaten those responsible for the vast mediocrity of most work in any medium.

Since May 6 is Welles's birthday, the perfect way to celebrate is by seeing his birth—fully formed—as one of the truly great filmmakers of the world. The complexity of this script and of the performances remain rare in pictures, and still seems fresh now, nearly sixty years after *Kane* was first seen. None of the leading players had ever appeared in a movie before, and nearly all of them here began long, rich careers: Joseph Cotten (as Kane's oldest friend), Everett Sloane (as Kane's most loyal employee), Ray Collins (as Kane's political nemesis), Agnes Moorehead (as Kane's beloved mother), Ruth Warrick (as Kane's first wife). Dorothy Comingore (as Kane's second wife) is so extraordinary that she held out for other roles this good, never found one, and was hardly seen again. If you look closely, you can spot Alan Ladd as a bit player in the last sequence. It is also the first amazing movie score by the brilliant Bernard Herrmann, whom Alfred Hitchcock would use on a number of his films, and whose scores improved many a picture. Herrmann had been discovered by Welles, who used him through most of his exceptional radio shows of the Thirties and Forties.

Of course, the most subversive aspect of *Citizen Kane*, in 1941 and now—because it is still relevant thematically and still devastating in its implications—is the dark light it throws on fame, success, wealth, and the heritage of plutocracy. Imagine how its negativity seemed to an American establishment about to enter World War II; its uncompromising picture of loneliness at the top is absolutely without any feature of redemption or spiritual survival. Impossible to think of an American film as essentially bleak in outlook, and yet the exhilarating freshness of its pace, wit, construction, and directorial style creates a kind of optimistic counterpoint, as if to say that only through the poetry of art can we hope to survive.

OTHER ORSON WELLES PICTURES:
   The Lady from Shanghai (1948; with Welles, Rita Hayworth, Everett Sloane).
   Mr. Arkadin (a.k.a. *Confidential Report*; 1955; with Welles, Paola Mori, Akim Tamiroff).
   Touch of Evil (1958; with Welles, Janet Leigh, Charlton Heston).
   The Trial (1962; with Welles, Anthony Perkins, Romy Schneider).

Also see Weeks 26 and 39.

BREAKFAST AT TIFFANY'S

L ast week (May 4) was Audrey Hepburn's birthday, and Mother's Day usually falls in this week, which is a perfect holiday to celebrate for Hepburn, who in her later years was a great mother-image to children the world over.

Audrey Hepburn was the studio system's last great female star, and she alone would justify its existence. In 1953, Hepburn won the best actress Oscar for her first starring role, in Paramount's William Wyler production *Roman Holiday*, and was the only actress among her 1950s contemporaries— Marilyn Monroe, Elizabeth Taylor, Grace Kelly, Ava Gardner—to survive as an adored star through the 1960s. Indeed, three of her most popular films were all released in that controversial transitional decade when the studio system collapsed and the "independent" Hollywood took over: *My Fair Lady* (1964), *Wait Until Dark* (1967), and probably— aside from *Roman Holiday*—the most defining role of her career, as Holly Golightly in Blake Edwards's 1961 romantic comedy-drama *Breakfast at Tiffany's*, loosely based on Truman Capote's short novel.

Hepburn's Holly has been perhaps the most often repeated image of her, not only in the years since her death in 1993, but long before. Hepburn played her last starring role in a feature in 1981 (in my romantic comedy, *They All*

Laughed), but in the final twenty years of her life she was most frequently represented as the free-spirited, unpredictable, and inimitably stylish Holly. In the movie, when she says "I love New York," you love it for all the magic she herself brings to the mythology of a great city. Blake Edwards, one of the best filmmakers of the last forty years, understood this profoundly while making *Breakfast at Tiffany's*; it's clear by the way he brings Hepburn into the film at the very beginning: an empty, early-dawn Fifth Avenue; a single cab; a tall, striking, unmistakable figure gets out, walks toward Tiffany's in a long shot, and Hepburn's title-card fades in, the "Moon River" theme playing with all the utter confidence of certain nostalgia.

From start to finish, Edwards knew it: this is Hepburn's picture, and he is never away from her for long. The rest of the cast give excellent support but aren't as memorable. George Peppard was never to be as good, retaining here an as-yet-unaffected, uncynically boyish laugh of delight with Hepburn. Patricia Neal couldn't have been thrilled with her Older-Woman-Paying-for-It part, but she brings to it a total freedom from sentimentality. Martin Balsam is guilelessly vulgar as a Hollywoodish New York agent. Buddy Ebsen is the equally unsentimentalized, not overly charming rural ex-husband of Holly.

But then there's the problem of Mickey Rooney doing his burlesque Japanese turn. Edwards himself recently expressed to me his discomfort with this, and certainly the performance is anything but politically correct today; indeed, the casting alone, by current standards, is unacceptable. And yet we don't object to Peter Sellers's aggressively vaudeville Frenchman as Inspector Clouseau in all of Blake Edwards's own *Pink Panther* series. Maybe, because of World War II, we are more sensitive to racist implications with Japanese than with French characters, but in fact Mickey's over-the-top impersonation is in an ancient show-business tradition of farcical ethnic caricatures and shouldn't really be judged too severely out of its own time.

Audrey Hepburn, however, is timeless. How beautifully she conveyed everything, and the subtle complications behind everything, and all with such amazing simplicity! Her silent looks, the grace and expressiveness of her movements, are a marvel. She is comparable in all those ways to the great women of the pre-talkie era—Lillian Gish, Mary Pickford, Gloria Swanson—in whose eyes you could read volumes. She shared with some of the early stars an abiding innocence, even when her character, like Holly, had been around. In life, Audrey was the most fragile, vulnerable person, and yet when she stepped in front of the camera, she would marshal all her fragility and vulnerability into an iron strength with which to express multiple nuances and colors. Her body paid a price, though, and she died much too young. The world she saw—from above in a man's Hollywood, or below on her brave UNICEF tours—was pretty bad, and yet the poetic dreamer in her could never be closed down. Audrey, the Dutch-English girl, is especially wonderful as a kind of self-invented American Southern girl in *Breakfast at Tiffany's*; when she sings "Moon River" with just a guitar, she could break your heart.

OTHER BLAKE EDWARDS COMEDIES:
Operation Petticoat (1959; with Cary Grant, Tony Curtis).
The Pink Panther (1964; with David Niven, Peter Sellers).
A Shot in the Dark (1964; with Peter Sellers).
What Did You Do in the War, Daddy? (1966; with Dick Shawn).
The Party (1968; with Peter Sellers).
Darling Lili (1970; with Julie Andrews, Rock Hudson).

The Return of the Pink Panther (1975; with Peter Sellers).
The Pink Panther Strikes Again (1976; with Peter Sellers).
Revenge of the Pink Panther (1978; with Peter Sellers).
10 (1979; with Dudley Moore, Julie Andrews, Bo Derek).
S.O.B. (1981; with Julie Andrews, William Holden).
Victor/Victoria (1982; with Julie Andrews, James Garner).
Skin Deep (1989; with John Ritter, Vincent Gardenia).

SWEET SMELL OF SUCCESS

"I'd hate to take a bite out of you, Sidney, you're a cookie full of arsenic" is one of numerous memorable lines in a brilliant American cult picture that is, with *Touch of Evil*, the last of the great films noir, and among the sharpest, most uncompromisingly dark Manhattan street movies—specifically of the old Times Square district—ever made: *Sweet Smell of Success*. An acidly etched drama of the gossip column–press agent world, the film was directed by Boston-born, Scotland-educated Alexander Mackendrick, who had been responsible for such classic British comedies as *Tight Little Island, The Man in the White Suit,* and *The Ladykillers*. This was his first American film, and was coproduced by its two stars, Burt Lancaster and Tony Curtis, both of them in (at the time) image-shattering roles which so disappointed their fans that the work, though fairly well received by critics, was a box-office disaster.

The original short novel and first-draft screenplay were by the savvy, talented Ernest Lehman, who would later write one of Alfred Hitchcock's best, *North by Northwest* (see Week 32), and who had himself been a New York City press agent, so that many of the often scabrous incidents came from hard-earned personal experience. The setup is simple: Lancaster—a powerful, Walter Winchell–like newspaper-TV gossip columnist named J. J. Hunsecker—has a latent

incestuous obsession with his younger sister; when she becomes serious about a jazz musician, he gets an ambitious
press agent called Sidney Falco to spread dirt on the fellow to
destroy him.

When Lehman became unavailable for revisions, Mackendrick surprised his producers by suggesting an old literary hero of his, 1930s boy-wonder playwright Clifford
Odets, then rather out of vogue. Odets—whose striking
plays *(Awake and Sing, Golden Boy)* had been famous for
idiosyncratic dialogue with a kind of larger-than-life street
vernacular that cut deep and resonated long—leapt at the
chance, keeping the basic plot and characters, but rewriting
everything else. Much of the picture's cult status is founded
on Odets's lines (in Barry Levinson's 1982 *Diner*, a character keeps quoting them). Curtis as Falco—in the most sear-
ingly unsympathetic characterization of his career, and
probably his finest—gets many of the best: ". . . Hunsecker's the golden ladder to the places I want to get," he
tells his secretary, "way up high, Sal, where it's always balmy,
and no one snaps his fingers and says, 'Hey, shrimp, rack
the balls' or 'Hey, mouse! mouse! go out and buy me a pack
of butts!' . . . From now on the best of everything is good
enough for me."

Lancaster, who had the "arsenic cookie" line above, is astonishingly grim and vicious, with no redeeming features;
he takes out a cigarette, says to Curtis: "Match me, Sidney."
Even the sadistic cop who calls Curtis "the boy with the ice-
cream face" has lines like "Come here, Sidney, I want to
chastise you." Lancaster's secretary comments, "You're so
immersed in the theology of making a fast buck." And the
poor cigarette girl, whom Curtis maneuvers to sleep with a
guy he wants a favor from, protests: "What am I, a bowl of
fruit—a tangerine that peels in a minute?"

All of this is played fast, thrown away nearly, through

Mackendrick's superbly paced direction, with camera work (by James Wong Howe) that is as flawless as it is evocative. *Sweet Smell of Success* only seems to get more modern with the years; a one-of-a-kind anomaly near the end of the studio system, it's a riveting, strangely disturbing masterpiece of mood, malice, and menace with mythic overtones in what Lancaster (as Hunsecker) describes as "a world of old rags and bones."

OTHER ALEXANDER MACKENDRICK PICTURES:

Tight Little Island (1949; with Joan Greenwood, James Robertson Justice).

The Man in the White Suit (1952; with Alec Guinness, Joan Greenwood).

The Ladykillers (1955; with Alec Guinness, Peter Sellers).

A Boy Ten Feet Tall (1963; with Edward G. Robinson).

A High Wind in Jamaica (1965; with Anthony Quinn, James Coburn).

STEAMBOAT BILL, JR.

In 1928, the last full year of nontalking pictures—and one of the two or three richest twelve-month periods of lasting banner films (like Week 47's *The Crowd*) in the history of movies—America's greatest and most physically beautiful comic talent, Buster Keaton, released probably his funniest work, the achingly hilarious *Steamboat Bill, Jr.* He cowrote, coproduced, codirected, and starred in it, but (unlike Charlie Chaplin, and as a kind of rebuke to him) took credit only as actor. In what would turn out to be his last independent picture—and the comedy climax of his career— Buster plays a pampered mama's boy who comes down South to meet and impress his macho riverboat-captain father (Ernest Torrence), whom he hasn't seen since he was an infant.

A couple of years ago, I watched this on the big screen with 750 men, women, and children, and I can't recall hearing that much laughter in years. It was so totally the smash hit of the 1997 Telluride Film Festival, this now seventy-one-year-old comedy, that it had to be rerun three times to accommodate demand. *Steamboat* is probably also Keaton's most smoothly consistent comic picture, with a spectacular hurricane-twister finale that is as awesome in technical brilliance as it is breathtakingly uproarious.

Remember, Keaton did all his own stunts, and *Steamboat*

features a virtual symphony of unbelievable falls. Yes, Buster didn't smile—his moniker in the 1920s was "the Great Stone Face"—but the variety of subtle expressions in all his movies is as memorably cinematic as his lithe and vividly expressive body. One comedy maxim of Keaton's, "You must always see a comedian's feet," is soundly exemplified in this brilliant masterwork of his mature flowering, which began in 1923 with his second feature film, *Our Hospitality,* and continued through such popular, superbly constructed and directed classics as *Sherlock, Jr.* and *The Navigator* (both 1924) and *The General* and *College* (both 1927). But every single one of his silent pictures is well worth seeing.

Born Joseph Francis Keaton in 1895, and having begun in show business at the tender age of about one, when his vaudeville-stumping parents put him into their brawling-couple comedy act, he acquired his new first name from legendary magician Harry Houdini. As part of their act, Keaton's father used to throw his young son at his wife; when the child was around three or four, someone in the audience was giving them a hard time, so Pa Keaton threw the little boy into the audience! After the show, Houdini, who had witnessed this, exclaimed: "That was some buster your kid took!" And so "Buster" became first a nickname and then eventually—after Keaton started in two-reel movies of 1917—the name of a world-famous star. Rotund comedian Fatty Arbuckle had initially featured him in his somewhat crude farces, but from 1920 to 1923, Keaton created a series of hugely successful, brilliantly funny shorts— like *One Week* (1920), *The Goat* and *The Boat* (both 1921), and *Cops* and *The Electric House* (both 1922)—before embarking on his extraordinary features. All of these are available currently, and undiminished in their inventiveness.

And *Steamboat Bill, Jr.* is a perfect example of Keaton's greatest qualities: deceptively simple, fast-paced, unpretentious, archetypically American. Every move he made had grace—even his wildest pratfall was a thing of beauty—and most of them are mind-boggling. Keaton was, finally, not only the purest, most unique, and strangely poetic of American comic artists, but also among the handful of the finest directors of comedy in world cinema. Long live Buster!

OTHER BUSTER KEATON FEATURES:
The Three Ages (1923; with Margaret Leahy, Wallace Beery).
Our Hospitality (1923; with Natalie Talmadge).
Sherlock, Jr. (1924; with Kathryn McGuire).
The Navigator (1924; with Kathryn McGuire).
Seven Chances (1925; with Ruth Dwyer).
Go West (1925; with Kathleen Myers).
Battling Butler (1926; with Sally O'Neil).
The General (1927; with Marion Mack).
College (1927; with Ann Cornwall).
The Cameraman (1928; with Marceline Day).

When writer–ex-G.I. Frank Sinatra (left) tells gambler-buddy Dean Martin that he's going to marry sometime-hooker Shirley MacLaine, Martin doesn't approve, calls her "a pig," in the first of numerous Sinatra-Martin pairings, and by far the best, Vincente Minnelli's complicated visualization of the James Jones novel, *Some Came Running* (Week 23).
Photo courtesy Photofest.

THE MAN WHO SHOT LIBERTY VALANCE

An appropriate way to celebrate Memorial Day (May 31) and the sacrifice of unknown soldiers: John Ford's 1962 Western drama, *The Man Who Shot Liberty Valance,* starring John Wayne, James Stewart, Vera Miles, and Lee Marvin. Not only Ford's elegiac final (artistically successful) look at the American West he had chronicled since his first films of 1917, it is also the last masterwork of the movies' golden age, which (as I see things) ended that same year.

Remarkably prophetic of the country's darkening future—Marilyn Monroe's mysterious death came that year, and John F. Kennedy's shocking murder the following year was only the first of the modern-day assassinations—the picture is, too, a complex variation on what Robert Graves called "the single poetic theme": a triangular love story of two men in love with the same woman.

Based on a Dorothy Johnson short story and starkly photographed in black and white, the tale is told almost entirely in flashback: Stewart plays an aged, much-loved Western senator who, with his wife (Miles), returns to the small town of Shinbone for the pauper's funeral of a forgotten rancher (Wayne). The local newspaper editor is naturally most curious as to why this distinguished American figure— known everywhere as "the man who shot Liberty Valance," a notoriously violent outlaw (Marvin)—has come all the way from Washington to pay his final respects to a man no one has heard of. Stewart tells him, and the story unfolds . . .

Years before, as an idealistic young pacifist attorney, Stewart had followed Tom Greeley's advice and gone west to help bring the law there. Robbed and brutally beaten by Valance, he is saved by Wayne, a prosperous young rancher, and nursed back to health by Wayne's intended, a local restaurant owner's feisty daughter (Miles), whom Stewart teaches to read and falls for in the process. This sets the stage for a complicated showdown between Wayne and Stewart, who are on opposite sides philosophically about the way order and law must be won, as well as being rivals in romance. Of course, there is also the showdown brewing between Marvin's vicious Valance and either Stewart or Wayne, a confrontation that finally, irrevocably, and ironically decides the outcome of the love triangle.

The truth of what really happened and how Liberty Valance actually did get shot and killed is considerably different from the legend we have been led to believe, but when the flashbacks are over, the newsman refuses to publish what he has been told, and he tells Stewart, as he tears up his article: "When the legend becomes fact, sir, print the legend." Yet we also come to understand that although Stewart and Miles have been married for decades, her truest love has remained with the man in the pine box she has come to bury.

None of this is spelled out in so many words, and I'm purposely not filling in the details so as to preserve the impact for those who haven't seen the movie. Suffice it to say that the ending and the way it is achieved have powerful emotional associations, not only within the picture itself but in its overall relationship to the whole of Ford's work.

Metaphorically, the film concludes with an America whose heroes are ambiguous or tainted, and whose yearning for the wilderness, for the time before frontiers were settled, remains its deepest passion.

The Man Who Shot Liberty Valance is not a young man's movie; it has the wisdom and poetic perceptions of an artist knowingly nearing the end of his life and career. Ford was sixty-seven when he made the picture, and he directed only a couple more, none with the personal intensity of this one. In the score, he even reprises a musical theme (by Alfred Newman) he had used over two decades earlier in his *Young Mr. Lincoln* (1939)—a theme that had movingly represented an unrequited love, something Ford understood profoundly since his own adoration of Katharine Hepburn in the late 1930s also had an unhappy ending.

All the performances are rich in archetypal reverberations. The entire cast helps to make this one of the glories of the American studio system, with whose collapse it not so coincidentally coincides.

OTHER JOHN FORD–JOHN WAYNE WESTERNS:
Stagecoach (1939; with Claire Trevor, Thomas Mitchell).
Fort Apache (1948; with Henry Fonda, Shirley Temple).
Three Godfathers (1949; with Pedro Armendáriz, Harry Carey Jr.).
She Wore a Yellow Ribbon (1949; with Joanne Dru, Ben Johnson, Harry Carey Jr.).
Rio Grande (1950; with Maureen O'Hara, Ben Johnson, Harry Carey Jr.).
The Searchers (1956; with Vera Miles, Jeffrey Hunter, Harry Carey Jr.).
The Horse Soldiers (1959; with William Holden, Constance Towers).

OTHER FORD–JAMES STEWART WESTERNS:

Two Rode Together (1961; with Richard Widmark, Shirley Jones).

Cheyenne Autumn (1964; with Richard Widmark).

OTHER FORD WESTERNS:

The Iron Horse (1924; with George O'Brien).

Three Bad Men (1926; with George O'Brien).

My Darling Clementine (1946; with Henry Fonda, Victor Mature).

Wagon Master (1950; with Ben Johnson, Harry Carey Jr.).

Sergeant Rutledge (1960; with Jeffrey Hunter, Constance Towers, Woody Strode).

Also see Weeks 11, 38, and 50.

SOME CAME RUNNING

In all the unprecedented outpouring of tributes to, reminiscences of, and commentaries on Frank Sinatra after his death, everyone, of course, mentioned his Oscar-winning performance in the 1953 adaptation of James Jones's novel *From Here to Eternity*. But only a handful singled out for special attention the other James Jones novel he was involved with for the screen, and yet it was a far more complicated and challenging role and certainly among the five best pictures Sinatra acted in: *Some Came Running*. In this 1959 color and CinemaScope small-town drama directed by Vincente Minnelli, Sinatra very convincingly plays a sometime writer—clearly a surrogate for Jones—who, after World War II, returns to his Indiana hometown, where he deals with the intensely conventional middle-class hypocrisy of his brother (a superb layered performance by Arthur Kennedy), and falls in love with a schoolteacher (well type-cast with Martha Hyer, though she is the weakest actor in the movie) who can explain artists to her students but cannot understand the one she sleeps with. The writer has an off-and-on affair with an ex-hooker (Shirley MacLaine in perhaps her most naked, heartbreaking performance) and becomes fast friends with a local gambler-boozer-playboy, whom Dean Martin incarnates (in one of his two best characterizations, the other being Howard Hawks's *Rio Bravo* of the same year).

This is one of those adult glossy Hollywood star pictures from the end of the golden age that, to be fully appreciated, should be given the same kind of close attention one would lavish on a foreign film. That is why so many European directors liked this movie: to them it *was* a foreign film. In Jean-Luc Godard's *Contempt* (see Week 41), released four years later, the French writer-character played by Michel Piccoli puts on a cowboy hat, and when his wife (Brigitte Bardot) asks him why he wears it in the bathtub, he refers her to Dean Martin's role in *Some Came Running*. Martin wears a cowboy hat throughout; indeed the hat is a running character-joke in the movie since Dean's superstitious gambler claims the hat is good luck and therefore never removes it, "even in bed," as one of his girlfriends says. The hat is beautifully paid off, by the way, in the final and most touching moment of the picture.

What makes the film so memorable—apart from all three stars working at peak believability—are the repeated ambiguities, the boxes within boxes, continually revealed about the characters by the script (meticulously adapted by playwright John Patrick) and by Minnelli's subtle camera placement and sensitive direction. None of the people in the story are quite what they seem to be, a reflection of the quality of the original source, Jones's underrated novel.

Knowing that Sinatra as a serious singer always did his recordings with full orchestra, did each song straight through, and normally required only one or two takes, Minnelli wisely staged nearly all the most important scenes in single continuous shots (which is why for maximum effect the movie should be seen in its original "letter-box" format). The single-shot technique also helps to give the work its acute sense of verisimilitude: there is no feeling of editorial manipulation, no interruption in the flow of what the actors are doing, of what the characters are experiencing. Scene after scene really happened exactly the way we are seeing them, only music (sometimes) has been added (from an extremely effective score by Elmer Bernstein). The players have to be really good, however, to work in this way, and they all are. Sinatra's role, in fact, is the least showy, but its central weight and complexity must be dead-on or the whole thing would collapse, and as an actor Sinatra has rarely been as focused or committed to the uneasy, never-black-and-white truth of his character. His presence here totally suspends disbelief, and carries a troubled unspoken inner gravity only a star actor can bring with such seeming effortlessness.

Overall, the picture is a darkly truthful piece of Americana, an honest and still contemporary look at our misogyny, anti-intellectualism, hypocrisy, and puritanism. Each of the characters is often wrong, but all of them are deeply human, and the stars are charismatic enough to make this resonate on a profoundly mythic level.

OTHER VINCENTE MINNELLI NONMUSICALS:
The Clock (1945; with Judy Garland, Robert Walker).
Father of the Bride (1950; with Spencer Tracy, Elizabeth Taylor, Joan Bennett).
The Bad and the Beautiful (1952; with Kirk Douglas, Lana Turner, Dick Powell, Gloria Grahame, Walter Pidgeon).
The Cobweb (1955; with Richard Widmark, Lauren Bacall, Charles Boyer, Gloria Grahame).
The Reluctant Debutante (1958; with Rex Harrison, Kay

Kendall, Sandra Dee).

Home from the Hill (1960; with Robert Mitchum, Eleanor Parker, George Hamilton, George Peppard).

Two Weeks in Another Town (1962; with Kirk Douglas, Edward G. Robinson, Cyd Charisse, Claire Trevor, George Hamilton).

The Courtship of Eddie's Father (1963; with Glenn Ford, Stella Stevens, Ron Howard).

Goodbye Charlie (1964; with Tony Curtis, Debbie Reynolds, Walter Matthau).

Also see Week 1.

ONLY ANGELS HAVE WINGS

If you haven't seen Cary Grant, Jean Arthur, and Rita Hayworth in Howard Hawks's romantic and exciting 1939 South American flying drama, *Only Angels Have Wings*, you have not experienced one of the most vibrant, resonant, and deeply entertaining movies ever made. It was the picture that took Grant from light-comedy star into the front ranks of leading men, the first successful dramatic film in which he got the girl, or rather, since it's Hawks, the girl got him. Grant impersonators always used to do him saying, "*Ju*-dy, *Ju*-dy, *Ju*-dy," which he actually never said in a film, but they got it from this movie: Rita Hayworth's character is named Judith, and Cary's typical pronunciation turns this into "*Ju*-dith." The picture also made Hayworth a star.

It is Hawks's first fully realized, extremely personal adventure story in what would come to be called the Hawksian tradition, a line traceable from this film to his 1944 *To Have and Have Not* with Humphrey Bogart (see Week 4) and his 1959 *Rio Bravo* with John Wayne. Indeed, Grant, Bogart, and Wayne in these three films seem to be Hawks's incarnations of a very similar guy at three very different ages—at his youngest and most vulnerable in *Only Angels Have Wings*, a poetically ambiguous title never explained or even alluded to in the film.

Set in a small seaport called Barranca, the story by

Hawks—one of the very few times he took a writing credit—revolves around a group of fliers at a tiny air transport company, flying mail and sometimes dangerous cargo through unpredictable weather over a hazardous mountain range. Grant runs the company for its owner, the Dutchman (well played by Sig Rumann), and his best friend is an aging aviator he calls Kid (a beautiful performance by Thomas Mitchell), while the love interest becomes a chorus girl who just happened to get off a boat for a look-see—not unlike the Lauren Bacall character in *To Have and Have Not*. She's played nicely here by that perennial good girl Jean Arthur, who resisted Hawks's attempts to make her sexually more provocative, and so the kind of sex antagonism he was to achieve with Ms. Bacall, or with Angie Dickinson in the same basic role in *Rio Bravo*, is not there. It exists far more vividly with Rita Hayworth, who turns out to have been Grant's nemesis a few years back. She left him because she couldn't handle living with his outrageously dangerous profession. In typical Hawks fashion, she ended up with another flier, touchingly played by the popular silent star Richard Barthelmess, who had been the lead in Hawks's first successful flying movie, *The Dawn Patrol* (1930; remade eight years later with a lot of Hawks footage and Errol Flynn). Barthelmess here plays a guy who had a terrible moment of cowardice, which caused his copilot's death.

When questioned on the inspiration for his characters in *Only Angels*, Hawks would say they were all based on people he had met or heard about in his own flying days—he used to build and fly airplanes as a youngster—and this contributes to the movie's strong sense of reality as well as to its richly personal quality, the dark aura of fatalism that hangs over it. Hawks's beloved younger brother, Kenneth Hawks (a promising director himself), had been killed in a flying accident a decade earlier. All the air sequences, therefore, have a most convincing intensity, a pervasive sense of the director's firsthand knowledge and passion for the profession, keenly felt as well in *The Dawn Patrol* and his two other exceptional flying pictures, *Ceiling Zero* (1935) and *Air Force* (1943).

The fast-paced, overlapping, offhand delivery of the lines; the moody, fog-enshrouded atmosphere; the oblique approach to the most dramatic moments; the almost religious ignoring of danger and death—all these are quintessentially Hawksian qualities, and this is one of his masterworks. It's also among my favorite movies, and I enjoy returning to its company far more often than to any of the other more famous releases from that same banner year, such as that old blockbuster, *Gone With the Wind*.

OTHER HOWARD HAWKS PICTURES:

A Girl in Every Port (1928; with Victor McLaglen, Louise Brooks).

The Dawn Patrol (1930; with Richard Barthelmess, Douglas Fairbanks Jr.).

Scarface (1932; with Paul Muni, George Raft).

Tiger Shark (1932; with Edward G. Robinson, Richard Arlen).

Ceiling Zero (1936; with James Cagney, Pat O'Brien).

Come and Get It (1936; with Edward Arnold, Frances Farmer, Joel McCrea, Walter Brennan).

Sergeant York (1941; with Gary Cooper, Joan Leslie, Walter Brennan).

Air Force (1943; with John Garfield, Gig Young, Arthur Kennedy, Harry Carey).

Red River (1948; with John Wayne, Montgomery Clift).

Also see Weeks 4, 29, and 42.

SINGIN' IN THE RAIN

There is simply no way around it: The 1952 Gene Kelly–Stanley Donen–Betty Comden–Adolph Green–Arthur Freed musical comedy about the movies, *Singin' in the Rain,* has proven the most thoroughly entertaining film-musical ever made. (And so it is a perfect way to celebrate the summer solstice, Midsummer Eve, and Midsummer Day.) There's nothing especially touching about it, as there is about *An American in Paris* (see Week 1), or bewitching like the early Ernst Lubitsch–Maurice Chevalier musicals (see Week 49), but there is also not one moment that isn't entirely delightful, nor one player who isn't a lot of fun to be with. Every single number is terrific, and the two most joyously optimistic musical sequences in pictures follow one another in the same reel: Kelly, Debbie Reynolds, and Donald O'Connor doing "Good Morning," and naturally Kelly's immortal "Singin' in the Rain," which is like a main-line injection of pure happiness.

The rarely-used-properly O'Connor achieves his own merry niche in the picture-musical hall of fame with his still uproariously charming slapstick paean to comedy-makers, "Make 'Em Laugh," an achievement in no way diminished by the fact that the tune and idea were shamelessly "borrowed" from Cole Porter's "Be a Clown," done four years earlier by Kelly in the 1948 Vincente Minnelli–Judy Garland period musical, *The Pirate*.

Speaking of borrowing: as Comden and Green genially admit, the general concept of the script as well as a number of specific jokes and ideas were inspired by the hilarious 1930 Moss Hart–George S. Kaufman Hollywood farce classic about the arrival of sound, *Once in a Lifetime* (the creating of which was the basis of Hart's lovely best-selling memoir, *Act One*). But, as Howard Hawks always advised, echoing an old show-business maxim, "Only steal from the best."

Kelly is satirically self-mocking, absolutely brilliant in his dancing, a charmer in his songs; O'Connor and Ms. Reynolds are both at their most likable; Jean Hagen certainly steals a good part of the show for laughs as the silent star with the impossibly shrill voice; and Millard Mitchell is the studio head of your dreams. The "Gotta Dance–Broadway Melody" ballet works well, too (except maybe for some of those billowing chiffon-dress moments with Cyd Charisse).

Overall, the picture is an original musical-comedy masterwork that has become a perennial favorite of audiences and critics (though strangely it was not an overwhelming success in its day). It is the most buoyant climax of a kind of national happiness that exploded in euphoric post–World War II optimism, memorialized by a series of musicals released between 1949 and 1954 (see Week 1). For pure simple fun, *Singin' in the Rain* is pretty tough to beat.

OTHER STANLEY DONEN–GENE KELLY MUSICALS:
> *Take Me Out to the Ball Game* (1949; with Frank Sinatra, Esther Williams, Jules Munshin; cowritten and choreographed by Donen and Kelly; directed by Busby Berkeley).

On the Town (1949; with Frank Sinatra, Vera-Ellen, Betty Garrett, Jules Munshin).

It's Always Fair Weather (1955; with Dan Dailey, Cyd Charisse, Michael Kidd).

OTHER DONEN MUSICALS:

Royal Wedding (1951; with Fred Astaire, Jane Powell, Peter Lawford).

Seven Brides for Seven Brothers (1954; with Howard Keel, Jane Powell; choreography by Michael Kidd).

Funny Face (1957; with Fred Astaire, Audrey Hepburn, Kay Thompson).

The Pajama Game (1957; with Doris Day, John Raitt, Carol Haney; codirected with George Abbott).

Damn Yankees (1958; with Gwen Verdon, Tab Hunter, Ray Walston; codirected with George Abbott).

Barbara Stanwyck is the tough, cynical newspaper reporter who essentially creates a false legend around Gary Cooper as an over-the-hill ballplayer supposedly wanting to protest the evils of the world by committing suicide in Frank Capra's antifascist drama, *Meet John Doe* (Week 27); but she falls for the guy, and he for her.
Photo courtesy The Kobal Collection.

THE MAGNIFICENT AMBERSONS

What Orson Welles did to the moneyed privileged class in *Citizen Kane* (see Week 18), he took to a more emotional level with the upper-middle-class Midwestern family of his second film, the equally audacious 1942 adaptation of Booth Tarkington's Pulitzer Prize–winning novel, *The Magnificent Ambersons*. This picture, however, coming on the heels of *Kane*'s financial failure and following two disastrous public previews, was savagely truncated by RKO Radio Pictures, with almost the entire last third dumped and partially reshot by others. That the film manages still to survive as a damaged but deeply disturbing and beautiful work, also often listed internationally as among the finest pictures ever made, only increases the terrible sense of loss one feels that the original can never be seen.

The first hour-plus of *Ambersons*, with certain omissions that are not crippling, shows the unique fluidity of the picture's portrait of an America now gone forever, destroyed essentially by the coming of the automobile; but the final twenty minutes—with nearly a half-hour deleted—is barely a ghost of what Welles had made. Nevertheless, I just saw it again recently and was overwhelmed by the profound impact with which the movie rewards a sensitive viewing.*

*A detailed breakdown of the original version of *The Magnificent Ambersons* can be found in my interview book with Welles, *This Is Orson Welles.*

Although Welles does not appear in *Ambersons*, he does narrate memorably—and several of those sequences contain lines of surpassing beauty—not only in the writing (from Tarkington's exquisite prose) but in the deeply resonant readings Welles gives the words. "The magnificence of the Ambersons began . . ." he starts over a black screen and then follows with one of the most unusual and effective openings in picture history, as he not only introduces with graceful economy all the major characters in the story but at the same time sets them evocatively in their period, in their fashions, in their community. "For nowadays," he tells us (the modern implications hanging in the air), "the faster we are carried, the less time we have to spare."

As we get into the tale, the narration diminishes, but it returns near the end for the climactic moments of leading character George Amberson Minafer's "comeuppance," which, Welles tells us, George got "three times filled and running over." It is, finally, the story of a young man's (Tim Holt) selfishness and a mother's (Dolores Costello) selflessness; of the coming of the automobile, as exemplified by the experiences of an inventor (Joseph Cotten); and of the end of an entire way of life, the end of an era.

For years, Welles tried to rescue and restore his *Ambersons*, but it was not to be, and it seems the footage was dumped into the Pacific Ocean in the late Fifties. It is, I think, the most tragic loss in all of film history. What remains—with exquisite, riveting performances from Cotten, Costello, Holt, and Anne Baxter (in her first picture), Agnes Moorehead (nominated for an Oscar that year), Ray Collins, Richard Bennett (father of Constance and Joan Bennett)—is so splendid that it gives a tantalizing idea of the virtuosity and genius of the missing material. (Despite the film's thoroughgoing failure upon initial release, the Academy nevertheless nominated it not only for

Moorehead's supporting performance, but for best picture, best photography, and best art direction.)

I remember sitting in a hotel room with Welles one time in the mid-1970s when *Ambersons* was on television and he accidentally flipped to it and then was forced by everyone in the room to watch reluctantly for a while. Though he tried to hide his emotion, tears came to his eyes. Later, when I asked him about the incident, he said that seeing what had been done to the movie only infuriated him, but what moved him was that "It's the past . . . it's over . . ." Ironically, this is the feeling that is engendered repeatedly as we watch his eloquent (no matter how damaged) chronicle of a lost time.

OTHER ORSON WELLES PICTURES:
The Immortal Story (1968; with Welles, Jeanne Moreau).
F for Fake (1975; with Welles, Oja Kodar).

Also see Weeks 18 and 39.

MEET JOHN DOE

In the Fifties and Sixties, my European parents would sometimes talk about the powerful antifascist theme—especially timely and valuable in 1941—expressed in Frank Capra's film of that year, *Meet John Doe*. They used to, at the same time, lament the loss of the kind of America that produced such a picture. (Perhaps this is a good thing to recall on Independence Day.)

Barbara Stanwyck gives one of her most richly complicated performances, as personable as it is honest, playing a success-hungry, outwardly cynical newspaper reporter who creates a fraudulent story about a would-be suicide—a protest against the iniquities of society—and then helps to cast her mock-martyr with a washed-up all-American ballplayer, now a hobo, incarnated with completely guileless charm and complexity by Gary Cooper in one of his most engaged, archetypal appearances.

Capra certainly had a way of getting persona-defining performances from star actors, like James Stewart in *Mr. Smith Goes to Washington* (1939) or Clark Gable in *It Happened One Night* (1934) or even Cooper himself five years earlier in the more popular but also more dated *Mr. Deeds Goes to Town* (1936). The director was personally fond of Stanwyck, who had starred in some of his early 1930s Columbia assignments, made before his ascension to the (then) low-budget studio's resident Oscar-winning wonder-boy genius with *It Happened One Night*, which won all the top four Academy Awards.

Indeed, Capra had a virtually unbroken string of hit pictures after this first sensation, with such popular works as his adaptation of James Hilton's *Lost Horizon* (1937) and his version of the George Kaufman–Moss Hart Pulitzer Prize–winning play, *You Can't Take It with You* (1938), which again won the best picture Oscar, though I've always felt it isn't as good as the original stage play. After a run like that, there had to be a dropping off, and Capra in the Forties and Fifties never really regained those giddy heights, though his first postwar movie, *It's a Wonderful Life* (1946)—a flop in its day—has become a Christmas perennial and among America's best-loved movies.

His first independent production was *Meet John Doe*, and he had trouble resolving its ending, finally relying on the effective, deeply emotional fireworks Stanwyck is able to produce with her final speech. Similarly, Cooper's unimpeachable believability lends credence to the plot of a nation entranced with a regular Joe's idealistic campaign. James Gleason as the newspaper editor, Edward Arnold as the main heavy, and Walter Brennan as Cooper's antiestablishment pal ("Look out for the Heelots!") are in the old Hollywood tradition of brilliant character support.

Capra used to say that if you played scenes at life's normal pace, they would seem slow; if you played them faster than normal, they would seem normal; if you played them faster than that, they would start to seem fast. Left over from his early comedy days, this maxim helps to keep his dramas fresh: he generally paced scenes very fast. It is impossible to separate Capra from the Americana of the period, and *Meet John Doe*, perhaps his darkest film, fatefully presages the dark war years ahead.

ANOTHER FRANK CAPRA–GARY COOPER PICTURE:
Mr. Deeds Goes to Town (1936; with Jean Arthur).

OTHER CAPRA PICTURES:
American Madness (1932; with Walter Huston).
Mr. Smith Goes to Washington (1939; with James Stewart, Jean Arthur, Claude Rains).
It's a Wonderful Life (1946; with James Stewart, Donna Reed).
State of the Union (1948; with Spencer Tracy, Katharine Hepburn).

Also see Week 45.

UGETSU

nternationally acknowledged as one of the towering works in world cinema, *Ugetsu* (1953) is probably the best known of Kenji Mizoguchi's eighty films. To the Japanese, Mizoguchi is far more representative of the East than Akira Kurosawa, with his more Western-influenced films, and therefore *Ugetsu* ranks high among Japan's most sublime artistic achievements and is, as well, one of the ten finest pictures made by anyone anywhere. And so it is especially fitting to commemorate the holy Japanese Day (July 17) in honor of the sun goddess Amaterasu.

The full title, *Ugetsu Monogatari,* means "Tales of a Pale and Shimmering Moon after the Rain," and the picture is, among other things, the most moving ghost story ever filmed, the only one I've ever seen that turns ghosts into living people in a fractured universe.

Set in sixteenth-century feudal Japan, *Ugetsu* follows two men—a potter (Masayuki Mori) and a merchant (Sakal Ozawa)—both of whom leave their loving wives and children in the self-centered, ambitious pursuit of glory, fame, and wealth. The potter eventually becomes involved with a beautiful phantom princess (Machiko Kyo), and the merchant achieves his goal of being a samurai, which he renounces only when he discovers that his wife (Mitsuko Mito) has been forced in his absence to become a prostitute.

The potter, after a fantasy of sexual pleasure, eventually becomes homesick and returns to find that his wife has been killed but—in one of the most moving, electrifying endings ever filmed—abides by him still, as a ghost.

Mizoguchi played many of his sequences in single, fluid shots that do not seem like created scenes so much as reality captured through a magical time machine. No other picturemaker in history could do in long shots—scenes shown from a distance—what Mizoguchi did repeatedly. Which is why the large screen is so important for the truest cinematic achievements: the reduction from the mythic size in which they were envisioned not only robs the artist of the scope of his canvas, but reduces everything to the level of a reproduction in a book or magazine (see discussion in the introduction). This is especially true with a subtitled film, and with Mizoguchi's amazing, often heartbreaking long shots— a kind of Japanese scroll in motion—capturing fluidly an epoch in history. The size helps to make the evocation resonate; the small screen not only loses impact but makes the viewing more of a strain. Nevertheless, for a masterwork like *Ugetsu*, the extra effort is worth it.

A hallmark of Mizoguchi's work was his extraordinary empathy with and understanding of women and their often subservient roles in society. As a child, he had seen his callous father's abuse of his mother and older sister, seen his sister sold off into the life of a geisha, suffered through his wife's madness brought on by syphilis. There are no films in history that portray with such sympathy the brutalizing, harrowing lives of women as *Ugetsu*, *The Life of Oharu* (1952), *Sansho the Bailiff* (1954), *The Princess Yang Kwei-Fei* (1955), and his final tragic *Street of Shame* (1956), known in England as *Red Light District*.

Afflicted from childhood with an eventually crippling rheumatism, Mizoguchi finally succumbed to leukemia at age fifty-eight, having been a director since he was twenty-four. At least fifty of his films have been lost, but the thirty-odd that remain, of which I have been able so far to see only a handful, place him securely among the immortals of the screen. With Jean Renoir in the West, Kenji Mizoguchi stands as the greatest of the East, a poet-painter of film at the highest level of achievement. As with only the finest art, his work is transcendent, enriches our lives, makes us better people.

OTHER KENJI MIZOGUCHI PICTURES:

Utamaro and His Five Women (1946).

The Life of Oharu (1952; with Kinuyo Tanaka, Toshiro Mifune).

Sansho Dayu/Sansho the Bailiff (1954; with Kinuyo Tanaka, Kyoko Kagawa).

Chikamatsu Monogatari/The Crucified Lovers (1954; with Kazuo Hasegawa, Kyoko Kagawa).

The Princess Yang Kwei-Fei (1955; with Masayuki Mori, Machiko Kyo).

Street of Shame (1956; with Machiko Kyo).

BRINGING UP BABY

The first time I saw Katharine Hepburn and Cary Grant (that was the billing) in Howard Hawks's delirious 1938 screwball romantic comedy, *Bringing Up Baby*, I was pretty sure it was the wildest, most outrageously funny talking picture I had ever seen. To make certain, I saw it again later that same day, early in 1961 when the movie was already twenty-two years old, and I was convinced. In fact, it was even funnier the second time. Of course I did see it on the big screen, which always makes a huge difference, but in this case even more so because of the film's extraordinary speed and the often darkly lit scenes, two things that can prove exhausting on the small screen. So be rested and on your toes.

I once asked Hawks if the lighting wasn't inordinately dark for a comedy and he drawled, with a grin, "Well, it was a complete tragedy for Cary, wasn't it?" He meant Grant's character, a paleontologist who has just lost a key bone to the brontosaurus he is assembling for the natural history museum he works with; he's lost it because of a superbly daffy society girl who has set her sights on him. She's played with absolutely dizzying charm by Hepburn in the single most likable performance of her career. Grant takes the thickly bespectacled absentminded professor about as far as you can go, yet is always entirely believable and hilarious in his helpless reaction to this female force of nature far

113

beyond that represented by any of the skeletal remains with which he generally deals. In her cupid's quiver, Hepburn's Susan has any number of pointed, if unknowing, assists from a rich aunt, wealthy friends, aggressive dog, and passive leopard. The "Baby" of the title, in fact, is the spotted leopard her aunt has acquired that is fond of music, in particular the song "I Can't Give You Anything But Love, Baby," which Kate and Cary sing to it once or twice as part of the lunatic circumstances of this uproarious adventure.

At one point, a slightly daft psychiatrist (Fritz Feld at his best) articulates the essential theme of the movie: "The love impulse in man often expresses itself in terms of conflict." The Hepburn-Grant relationship here perfectly illustrates this throughout. I didn't know until recently (from Barbara Leaming's Hepburn biography) that Hawks and screenwriter Dudley Nichols were inspired in the creation of this movie by the lovingly antagonistic relationship between Hepburn and thickly bespectacled master director John Ford during the making in 1936 of *Mary of Scotland*, for which Nichols had also served as scenarist. Hepburn was the only person who had ever managed to kid Ford on the set and get away with it, and her own strong-mindedness matched his. They fell in love, Ford nearly left his wife and kids for her, but it wasn't to be. *Bringing Up Baby* cheerfully takes this real relationship to farce level and gives it a happy ending.

For Hawks, the picture was actually about the breaking down of a hung-up guy. By the end, Grant's character realizes that even though he seemed to be having the worst time, it was actually liberating and made him a larger human being; indeed the film is a series of tests Grant must undergo to be worthy of a beautiful woman as adorable as Hepburn. Only a partial success in its day, and forgotten for years, *Bringing Up Baby* is among my most favorite pictures, and one of the great comic treasures of the American screen.

OTHER HOWARD HAWKS–CARY GRANT COMEDIES:
  His Girl Friday (1940; with Rosalind Russell, Ralph Bellamy).
  I Was a Male War Bride (1949; with Ann Sheridan).
  Monkey Business (1952; with Ginger Rogers, Marilyn Monroe, Charles Coburn).

Also see Week 24.

OTHER HAWKS COMEDIES:
  Fig Leaves (1926; with George O'Brien, Olive Borden).
  Ball of Fire (1942; with Gary Cooper, Barbara Stanwyck).
  Gentlemen Prefer Blondes (1953; with Marilyn Monroe, Jane Russell).
  Man's Favorite Sport (1964; with Rock Hudson, Paula Prentiss).

Also see Weeks 4 and 42.

THE THIRD MAN

One of the best and still freshest of films noir is 1949's *The Third Man*. Like *Casablanca*, it is a classic example of a most memorable picture that represents not really the personal vision of one artist, but rather an amazingly fortuitous convergence of talents at just the right moment with exactly the correct material, all working, both separately and together, at top form. The idea for the movie—an American writer trying to unravel his friend's mysterious death in a corrupt post–World War II Vienna run by all four Allied forces—came from the brilliant, legendary Hungarian producer (and sometime studio head and director) Alexander Korda.

Korda took it to one of England's finest contemporary novelists, Graham Greene—not only an excellent prose and dialogue writer but a superb constructionist. Greene did the original screenplay, although the most famous speech in the picture was actually contributed (as acknowledged in the published Greene screenplay) by one of its stars, Orson Welles as the mysterious Harry Lime.

LIME [to Holly Martins, played by Joseph Cotten].
. . . And don't be so gloomy. . . . After all, it's not that awful—you know what the fellow said: In Italy for thirty years under the Borgias they had warfare,

terror, murder, bloodshed—they produced Michel-
angelo, Leonardo da Vinci, and the Renaissance. In
Switzerland they had brotherly love, five hundred
years of democracy and peace, and what did that produce? . . . The cuckoo clock.

As a P.S., Welles told me: "When the picture came out, the
Swiss very nicely pointed out to me that they've never made
any cuckoo clocks—they all came from the Schwarzwald, in
Bavaria!"

Welles's role of Harry Lime is one of the briefest leading
parts in any movie, yet it dominates the picture and is its
most unforgettable aspect. Welles always used to say it was a
"perfect star part," like the title role in the famous old stage
melodrama, *Mister Wu*. "All the characters," Orson said,
"boil around the stage for about an hour shrieking, 'What
will happen when Mr. Wu arrives?' . . . and so on. Finally, a
great gong is beaten, and slowly over a Chinese bridge
comes Mr. Wu himself . . . a lot of coolies yell, 'Mr. *Wu*!'
The curtain comes down, the audience goes wild, and
everyone says, 'Isn't that guy playing Mr. Wu a great actor!'
That's a star part for you!" (It is also the only screen role of
Welles's entire career that he did with absolutely no
makeup, especially no false nose.) However, it is also un-
questionable that director Carol Reed's extremely effective
style of shooting and cutting this picture would have been
inconceivable prior to director Welles's earlier films, *Citizen
Kane, The Stranger,* and *The Lady from Shanghai*.

At the head of a flawless cast of European actors is
Welles's own discovery, Joseph Cotten, at his most amiable,
with Alida Valli at her most alluring and Trevor Howard at
his most acerbic. The famous theme music, all composed
and played on a zither, became an international pop hit.

In America, the film was bought for distribution by

producer David O. Selznick, who, though he'd had nothing to do with its making, slapped his name all over the credits. A year later, Selznick, Korda, and Welles were at Cannes, Orson told me, and Korda suddenly said to Selznick: "You know, David, I just hope I don't die before you." Surprised, Selznick asked why. Korda replied: "Because I hate to think of you going to my gravestone, scratching off my name, and putting yours on instead."

OTHER CAROL REED PICTURES:

Bank Holiday (*Three on a Weekend;* 1938; with John Lodge, Margaret Lockwood).

The Stars Look Down (1939; with Michael Redgrave, Margaret Lockwood).

Night Train to Munich (1940; with Rex Harrison, Margaret Lockwood, Paul Henreid).

Kipps (1941; with Michael Redgrave, Diana Wynyard).

The Young Mr. Pitt (1942; with Robert Donat, Robert Morley).

Odd Man Out (1947; with James Mason, Robert Newton).

The Fallen Idol (1948; with Ralph Richardson, Michele Morgan).

Outcast of the Islands (1951; with Trevor Howard).

The Man Between (1953; with James Mason).

A Kid for Two Farthings (1955; with Celia Johnson, Diana Dors).

Trapeze (1956; with Tony Curtis, Burt Lancaster).

The Key (1958; with William Holden, Sophia Loren).

Our Man in Havana (1959; with Alec Guinness, Burl Ives, Maureen O'Hara, Noel Coward).

The Running Man (1963; with Laurence Harvey, Lee Remick).

Cary Grant is a complaisant, successful Madison Avenue executive at the start of Alfred Hitchcock's roller-coaster thriller, *North by Northwest* (Week 32), but pretty soon he's been mistaken for a government agent, kidnapped, almost killed, arrested for drunken driving, hunted for murder, and duped into a fateful meeting with a vengeful crop duster; script by Ernest Lehman.

Photo courtesy Photofest.

OPEN CITY

I once asked Jean Renoir what he thought of his own early talking picture, *Boudu Saved from Drowning* (1932), and he said: "Oh, well, the sound is not so good, and the film stock kept changing so the photography certainly is not perfect and the camera work is sometimes very rough; the music is not well recorded, and in the cutting, some shots are too long and some are too short, but I think perhaps it is my best picture."

This pithy comment on talent over technical perfection is called to mind by the raw power of Roberto Rossellini's first major film and one of the first Italian post–World War II pictures, 1945's hard-hitting *Open City (Roma, Città Aperta)*. A brutally honest look at the travails of some of the Italian underground in Nazi-occupied Rome, Rossellini's film changed movies forever. Though Renoir himself had shot on real locations not only in *Boudu* but with nonprofessional actors in *Toni* (1935), no one had taken to the streets with amateurs quite so fully as Rossellini did with *Open City* and its companion piece *Paisan* (1946).

Of course, some of the players were pros, like the tough-tender Aldo Fabrizi as a courageous priest—and, of course, the legendary Anna Magnani. In fact, if there is a better performance—more naked, more overwhelmingly real—than Magnani's in this picture, I can't think of it. She is simply breathtaking. Without Renoir and Rossellini, by the way, today's entire independent movement would not exist; they pointed the way for all time: Tell the truth.

With a script cowritten by Rossellini and Federico Fellini, and an exceptional musical score by the director's brother Renzo Rossellini, *Open City*, though not very much admired at first in its native Italy, made a tremendous impression in France and the United States, creating a vogue in art houses for Italian cinema, coining the genre known as neorealist, even starting a trend of gritty documentary-style pictures in Hollywood that went from the late Forties into the early Fifties. Features like *13 Rue Madeleine* (1946), *Boomerang* (1947), *The Street With No Name* (1948), *Call Northside 777* (1948), and numerous others would never have happened without the lead of *Open City*. But no other film ever matched its rough, edgy, angry power.

Essentially a series of episodes of ever-escalating intensity in the covert hostilities between the Italian Resistance and the Nazi Gestapo, the picture builds suspense in seemingly improvised fashion, with an effect of artlessness that somehow is achieved invisibly. Rossellini's other World War II films, *Paisan* and *Germany Year Zero*, while effective, do not quite manage the hypnotic, inexorable flow of *Open City*.

This period was followed by a disastrous series of seven exceedingly personal, and occasionally sublime, films with Ingrid Bergman, who left her marriage and Hollywood career to share her life and work with Rossellini in a "scandalous" liaison. The best of these movies, *Europa '51* and *Voyage to Italy*, are considered by hip film aficionados as among the finest of world cinema, but Rossellini did not achieve box-office success again until he returned once more to World War II as his subject, with 1959's powerful *General Della Rovere*, starring Vittorio De Sica, who, as director, had been at the forefront of the Italian neorealist movement with his *Shoeshine* (1946) and *The Bicycle Thief* (1948).

But *Open City* remains the defining tragic work of this extraordinary moment in picture history, one that reverberates to this day in the films of directors who try to put real life vibrantly on the screen.

OTHER ROBERTO ROSSELLINI PICTURES:

Paisan (1946; with Carmela Sazio, Dots Johnson, Robert Von Loon, Maria Midri).

Germany Year Zero (1948; with Edmund Meschke, Ernst Pittschau, Ingetraud Hintze).

Stromboli (1949; with Ingrid Bergman, Mario Vitale).

Europa '51/The Greatest Love (1952; with Ingrid Bergman, Alexander Knox).

Viaggio in Italia/Strangers (1953; with Ingrid Bergman, George Sanders).

Fear (1954; with Ingrid Bergman, Kurt Kreuger).

General Della Rovere (1959; with Vittorio De Sica, Hannes Messemer, Sandra Milo).

NORTH BY NORTHWEST

For 1959, when the William Wyler–Charlton Heston biblical epic *Ben-Hur* won eleven Oscars including best picture, there were some of us who felt quite strongly that the best American movie of the year was either the Howard Hawks–John Wayne Western, *Rio Bravo,* or the Alfred Hitchcock–Cary Grant thriller, *North by Northwest.* Some of us still do. In fact, I would bet money that if the three films were playing side by side, there would be far more walkouts on the Wyler than on the Hawks or the Hitchcock. (The only way I could advise people to watch *Ben-Hur* would be to sit through the beginning to get the idea, then go out for lunch and come back in time for the chariot race, which was magnificently staged and directed by former stuntman Yakima Canutt.)

I remember seeing *North by Northwest* for the first time nearly forty years ago at a running for the New York press in the old MGM screening room, and being bowled over by the film's absolutely mesmerizing ride from the streets of Manhattan to the flats of Illinois to the Mount Rushmore monument at Rapid City, South Dakota. Simply, it has to be Hitchcock's most consistently delightful entertainment, the ultimate expression of one of the director's main themes, the perils of complacency. And it is the climax not only of Hitchcock's trio of innocent-man-on-the-run pictures—which began with his best English film, *The 39 Steps* (1935), and continued with the more darkly wartime *Saboteur* (1942)—but also of his elegant suspense-comedy-sex mixtures, of which *Rear Window* (1954) is another high point. However, *Rear Window* essentially plays in one room and a courtyard while *North by Northwest* goes all over the United States and comes full circle back to England, with two British-born actors, Cary Grant and James Mason, as hero and heavy. The casting in itself is a typically wicked Hitchcockian joke, since Grant was a much bigger star than Mason, but during their lifetime, Mason was considered the far better actor.

When I first met Hitchcock early in 1961, only two years after *North by Northwest* had been a huge financial success (I saw it again at the sixty-five-hundred-seat Radio City Music Hall, where it opened exclusively in New York and broke records), he was still irritated by some of the critical reactions. He scoffed as he mentioned that the *New Yorker* critic had said his film was "unconsciously funny." Hitchcock shook his head. "Can you imagine?" he asked, incredulous. "Why, it's an absolute fantasy. Even the title doesn't exist: there is no such reading on a compass as north by northwest." Hitch was also completely overlooked at the Oscars, even in nominations, and although *North by Northwest* was an extremely profitable picture, Cary Grant's other movie that year, a light service comedy called *Operation Petticoat* (produced by Grant, directed by Blake Edwards), was the highest grossing film in Grant's career.

Obviously *North by Northwest* is not as effective on the tube, since the bravura virtuosity of Hitchcock's work needs every inch of its beautifully color-photographed Vista-Vision space. Arguably, with John Ford's *The Searchers* (1956), this was the best VistaVision movie in the best wide-screen process ever invented—and now used only for certain trick shots. The film looks so fresh you forget how many imitations and wanna-bes it spawned, and you feel yourself to be in the presence of an original. It's the most likable culmination of the Hitchcock-Grant collaborations, their fourth, begun superbly with *Suspicion* (1941), followed brilliantly with *Notorious* (see Week 8), and romantically by *To Catch a Thief* (1955). Classic sequence follows classic sequence, all smoothly piloted by Ernest Lehman's clever, tightly dialogued script: the abduction at the Plaza, the train ride, the crop duster, the auction, the escape over Lincoln's nose at Mount Rushmore. Bernard Herrmann's score is magnificent. Eva Marie Saint is terrific in the one sexy glamour role of her distinguished career; James Mason and Martin Landau are both excellent. But it's Cary's picture start to finish, and you wouldn't want it any other way. If you've never seen *North by Northwest*, you are in for one of the most enjoyable rides in picture history. Among my absolute favorites.

OTHER ALFRED HITCHCOCK–CARY GRANT PICTURES:
See Week 8.

OTHER HITCHCOCK INNOCENT FUGITIVE/GUILT TRANSFERENCE PICTURES:
The 39 Steps (1935; with Robert Donat, Madeleine Carroll).
Saboteur (1942; with Robert Cummings, Priscilla Lane).
I Confess (1953; with Montgomery Clift, Anne Baxter, Karl Malden).
The Wrong Man (1957; with Henry Fonda, Vera Miles).
Frenzy (1972; with Jon Finch, Alec McCowen, Barry Foster, Anna Massey).

Also see Week 15.

ROBIN HOOD

Just to give an idea of the now nearly unfathomable worldwide popularity of Douglas Fairbanks (1883–1939): When he and his bride, the equally popular Mary Pickford ("America's Sweetheart"), went on a European honeymoon, they found themselves literally unable to leave their hotels in Paris, London, and Rome because of the crowds out front, day and night, hoping for a glimpse of gods momentarily come down to earth. Remember, the lack of sound not only contributed to all silent film stars' mystery, but also made them instantly universal, mythically resonant in every country, because by speaking no words, they spoke all languages.

Douglas Fairbanks was the first international American movie hero, and he represented for millions around the globe the idea of what an American was: bold, brash, outgoing, youthfully super-agile, with great good humor. He became famous for his athletic prowess and grace, and for doing all his own jumps, leaps, climbs, and stunts.

The boyhood idol of actor-filmmakers as disparate as Orson Welles and Laurence Olivier, Fairbanks had many who emulated him—from Errol Flynn to Burt Lancaster to Kevin Kline and even, once or twice, Douglas Fairbanks Jr. Born in Colorado, Fairbanks was also the first Western film star—numerous Fairbanks features (1915–1919) were set

in the West or he played a Westerner in the East—this being often forgotten since, starting in 1920, he veered almost
entirely into phenomenally successful swashbucklers, like
the originals of both *The Mark of Zorro* (1920) and *The
Three Musketeers* (1921). His third blockbuster of this kind
was the first picture in history to cost one million dollars; it
was, as well, Fairbanks's ninth collaboration with pioneer
Toronto-born master Allan Dwan (1885–1981), who persuaded the reluctant Doug to star in 1922's *Robin Hood*.

Fairbanks had been resisting his partners' urgings to play
this role, saying he didn't want to be "a flat-footed Englishman walking through the woods." But Dwan—a former
Notre Dame football star and already a veteran of some of
Fairbanks's best and most successful early works (like *Manhattan Madness* from 1916 or *Bound in Morocco* from
1918)—persuaded him, first by getting him hooked on
bows and arrows. Later, when the actor was frightened by
the stolidity of the ninety-foot walls of their castle, Dwan
did a couple of Fairbanks-type stunts, sliding down a curtain and jumping onto a wall to show off the possibilities.

In fact, Dwan had a great many qualities in common
with Fairbanks's persona: physical prowess, a sense of joy, an
absence of pomposity, a fondness for people. Talking about
directors who were good, Howard Hawks once said to me:
"Allan Dwan I admired. He was a pro—tough and hard
with a good touch. He didn't dwell on things—he just hit
'em and went on." The pacing of *Robin Hood*, with its extraordinary sets and crowd scenes, is slower than the average
early Fairbanks, but you also have to make sure the picture
is being projected at the right speed: a slowed-down *Robin
Hood* is interminable, a sped-up one is ridiculous. The
silents had no fixed speed (as sound speed is fixed at twenty-
four frames per second) and for years fluctuated essentially
between sixteen and twenty-two frames per second; but a

few frames make a huge difference in the effect of the work today. That and print quality (usually poor) and musical accompaniment (often bad) make seeing silent films correctly very difficult.

Dwan was the loveliest old gentleman when I knew him—ages eighty to ninety-six—still jovial, deeply encouraging, understanding, funny. He gave me the best definition for what made "certain people" uniquely film stars, something that didn't exist before Douglas Fairbanks, America's most popular star during World War I and through the Twenties. "In pictures, personalities are it," Dwan said. "It isn't acting per se as it's known in the theater. You'd bring some kid in who just blazed off the screen. . . . That's what we looked for—some photographic quality, some mysterious hidden thing certain people have. . . ."

OTHER ALLAN DWAN–DOUGLAS FAIRBANKS PICTURES:
   The Habit of Happiness (1916; with Dorothy West).
   The Good Bad Man (1916; with Bessie Love).
   The Half-Breed (1916; with Alma Rubens).
   Manhattan Madness (1916; with Jewel Carmen).
   A Modern Musketeer (1917; with Marjorie Daw).
   Mr. Fix-It (1918; with Wanda Hanley).
   Bound in Morocco (1918; with Pauline Curley).
   He Comes Up Smiling (1918; with Marjorie Daw).
   The Iron Mask (1929; with Marguerite de la Motte).

OTHER DWAN PICTURES:
   Manhandled (1924; with Gloria Swanson).
   Stage Struck (1925; with Gloria Swanson).
   While Paris Sleeps (1932; with Victor McLaglen).
   Heidi (1937; with Shirley Temple).
   The Three Musketeers (1939; with Don Ameche, the Ritz
      Brothers).
   Frontier Marshal (1939; with Randolph Scott).

Up in Mabel's Room (1944; with Dennis O'Keefe).
Brewster's Millions (1945; with Dennis O'Keefe).
Rendezvous with Annie (1946; with Eddie Albert).
Sands of Iwo Jima (1949; with John Wayne).
Tennessee's Partner (1955; with Ronald Reagan, John Payne).
The River's Edge (1957; with Ray Milland, Anthony Quinn).

ARTISTS AND MODELS

Orson Welles said that high among the most hilarious things he'd ever seen was the team of Dean Martin and Jerry Lewis when they performed in nightclubs, which is how the act first became popular between 1945 and 1949—the year they played in their first movie. "You have no idea how funny they were!" Orson said. "You'd pee your pants."

Jerry and Dean—in terms of the brains behind the act, that would have been the billing—broke up the places, like New York's Copacabana where they were a sellout smash every time they played. When Martin tried to sing, Lewis disrupted and erupted. They fought, did falls, ran into the audience, took people's steaks, and cut people's ties. Fans screamed and couldn't get enough.

Both Dean and Jerry were savvy, sexy, young, attractive, tall, and agile. Dean was a witty, crooner-mocking singer, Jerry perhaps the most savagely belly-laugh-funny comedian of the last fifty years.

Of course, all those live performances—later, their stage appearances at the old Paramount became legendary—are only there in the memories of those who were lucky enough to see them. Second best are those absolutely live, no tape-ahead television shows Martin and Lewis did between 1949 and their breakup in 1955. Recently I saw a bunch of their old *Colgate Comedy Hour*s and much was still fall-down-on-the-floor hilarious. Third best are their movies, two supporting-role appearances, and fourteen starring-role musical comedies that were way up there among the biggest moneymakers of the Fifties. There are good moments in most of them, but only two, both directed by Frank Tash-lin, hold together as movies: their best, *Artists and Models* (1955); and their last as a team, *Hollywood or Bust* (1956).

Tashlin—formerly a cartoonist, a cartoon director at Warner Brothers, a screenwriter, and a cult-favorite of the French New Wave—was the perfect filmmaker for Martin and Lewis, exploiting their often cartoonish, musical-comedy personalities in a satirical context, first with kids' horror comic books as the butt of the humor, then with Hollywood fans (short for *fanatics*). *Artists and Models* is especially cutting and still as relevant in its garish look at the world of bloody children's horror comics. Tashlin's colors were often outrageous, but that was the point: it was like an only slightly exaggerated reflection of the audience's taste. Tashlin would eventually direct six of Lewis's most success-ful solo pictures, and he encouraged the comedian's own di-recting career; Jerry always referred to him as "my teacher."

Tashlin was the first to notice what he used to call Dean Martin's "Cary Grantish abilities," and he created numbers around him that were very flattering, and which Martin pulls off extremely well. Jerry Lewis was given formidable female competition in a young dancer-singer named Shirley MacLaine, whom Lewis (with producer Hal Wallis) had first seen on Broadway. This became MacLaine's second movie; in one amazing musical number on a flight of stairs, she and Lewis outdo each other to the death. Dean's vis-à-vis is a Vegas-glamorous Dorothy Malone. The boys have a charming sentimental number together, "Pretend," and there's a rousing finale at the Artists and Models ball. You can tell that one of Tashlin's favorite films was Howard Hawks's gaudy musical *Gentlemen Prefer Blondes* of two years earlier.

On the entire shoot of *Hollywood or Bust*, Tashlin told me, Martin and Lewis did not speak to each other except in their scenes together. "It was a bitch," Tashlin said. You can't really tell in the movie, though obviously it doesn't have the freshness of the earlier film. One of Tashlin's other favorite directors was Ernst Lubitsch (see Weeks 12, 49, 52), and there's a pleasant musical sequence, "A Day in the Country," that is an homage to Lubitsch's famous "Beyond the Blue Horizon" romantic-satiric sequence in *Monte Carlo* (1930), where all the farmers and country people wave to the passing train; here it's all Vegas showgirls dressed in scanty rural outfits. Tashlin wanted to preface the sequence with a shot of the car going by a county sign reading YOU ARE NOW ENTERING LUBITSCH, but the studio took that out. Of course I first saw these movies in my mid-teens when I was an unequivocal fan of Martin and Lewis, so I do admit to nostalgic attachments.

OTHER FRANK TASHLIN–JERRY LEWIS PICTURES:
  Rock-a-Bye Baby (1958; loosely adapted from Preston Sturges's
    The Miracle of Morgan's Creek).
  It's Only Money (1962; with Zachary Scott).
  Who's Minding the Store? (1963; with Jill St. John, Agnes
    Moorehead).
  The Disorderly Orderly (1964; with Glenda Farrell, Susan
    Oliver).

OTHER TASHLIN PICTURES:
  Son of Paleface (1952; with Bob Hope, Jane Russell, Roy
    Rogers).

The Girl Can't Help It (1956; with Tom Ewell, Jayne Mansfield).

Will Success Spoil Rock Hunter? (1957; with Tony Randall, Jayne Mansfield).

Bachelor Flat (1962; with Terry-Thomas).

The Alphabet Murders (1966; with Tony Randall, Robert Morley).

The Glass Bottom Boat (1966; with Doris Day).

Walter Matthau is a penniless
playboy who decides to marry a
bookish botanist who's also an
heiress, Elaine May, and then
do away with her and collect
the large inheritance, but his
plans go awry in *A New Leaf*
(Week 36), also written and
directed by Ms. May; indeed,
she nearly kills him with love.
Photo courtesy Photofest.

GASLIGHT

One of those movies that keep getting better and strangely more relevant as years go by is George Cukor's brilliantly suspenseful adaptation—starring Ingrid Bergman, Charles Boyer, Joseph Cotten, and Angela Lansbury (in her first role)—of Patrick Hamilton's successful stage melodrama, originally titled *Angel Street*, released in 1944 as *Gaslight*. To those who've seen this superbly acted psychological murder story in which a husband (Boyer) systematically tries to drive his wife (Bergman) insane, the phrase "to *Gaslight*" a person—a variant of playing "mind games"—carries a shiver of recognition: How often do we find ourselves being manipulated by others' attempts to bend us to their will? The husband's single-minded assault is only a homicidally extreme form of a horribly common human trait: twisting or altering truth to accommodate selfish needs. The process can lead to a kind of vicious psychological abuse every bit as destructive as the more obvious physical kind. In *Gaslight*, Bergman and Boyer become a sort of mythic incarnation of the millennia-old destruction of women by men, through the insidious use against her of the female's most constructive impulses of compassion and trust.

The picture has such modern reverberations that it is surprising to note how early in the Forties it was made; it feels

in its intensity more like a later noir variation. Boyer's amazing French charm and authority are used to diabolical effect: a part of you doesn't want to believe he could be so heartlessly cruel. Playing this against Bergman, still at her most romantically virginal—remember, this is right after *Casablanca* (1943) and her second smash, *For Whom the Bell Tolls* (1944), where she asks Gary Cooper how to kiss: "Where do the noses go?"—makes for a potent result; when she finally has her revenge, you are absolutely as bloodthirsty as she has become. No wonder she received for this performance her first of two Oscars for best actress, nor that the work was nominated for seven other Academy Awards: best picture, best actor (Boyer), best screenplay (mainly done by playwright John Van Druten, with help from earlier drafts by Walter Reisch and John L. Balderston), best supporting actress (Lansbury), best photography, and best sets and decor, for which it also won, with a haunting evocation of the late gaslight period in London.

Angela Lansbury was seventeen and wrapping Christmas presents at Bullocks when she was recommended by scenarist Van Druten (who had met her with her British actress mother) for the "very good part of a rather sluttish housemaid," as Cukor described the role to me. The director went on about Lansbury: "The very first day on the set, she was absolutely at home—she had never acted—and she was an actress. . . . She had the talent for changing herself physically without appearing to. And she had this rather sullen, bad-tempered face—rather impertinent face—it just came from the inside. And there was this full-blown character."

Of course, Cukor was a magnificent director of new talent—Katharine Hepburn, Jack Lemmon, Judy Holliday, Shelley Winters, and Vivien Leigh all did their first movies with him. He was also an extraordinary enabler of stars— Greta Garbo, Jean Harlow, Judy Garland, Cary Grant, and

Ronald Colman gave some of their greatest performances under Cukor's steady hand and discerning eye. He had an uncanny gift for bringing out the best in his actors through his often earthy honesty and candor, his refusal to accept less than the finest, less than truth.

Although the back story about the wife's murdered opera-singer aunt and the hidden jewels is pure old-fashioned mystery melodrama, and Cotten's character of the civilized cop is not fully realized in the writing, *Gaslight* nevertheless ranks high in the life achievements of Cukor, Bergman, Boyer, Lansbury, and MGM—it's a much darker vision of life than the lion's roar would usually precede—and it is still one of the most troubling pictures ever made dealing with the battle of the sexes, to my mind the single most important war still waging worldwide.

OTHER GEORGE CUKOR DRAMATIC PICTURES:
David Copperfield (1935; with Freddie Bartholomew, W. C. Fields).
Camille (1937; with Greta Garbo, Robert Taylor, Lionel Barrymore).
A Double Life (1947; with Ronald Colman, Signe Hasso, Shelley Winters).
A Star Is Born (1954; with Judy Garland, James Mason).
Heller in Pink Tights (1960; with Sophia Loren, Anthony Quinn).

Also see Weeks 7 and 51.

A NEW LEAF

In the early Seventies, while us guys—John Cassavetes, Mike Nichols, Bob Rafelson, Warren Beatty, Francis Coppola, Jack Nicholson, Woody Allen, Dennis Hopper, Billy Friedkin, Marty Scorsese, Steven Spielberg, George Lucas, and others—were changing American pictures, there was also one gal: Elaine May. She wrote, directed, and costarred (with Walter Matthau) in her first film, released in 1971. Quite popular then, it remains one of the glories of New or Old Hollywood, a comedy classic in its own time: *A New Leaf.* The picture wasn't just funny, meaningful, superbly paced, and always photographed from exactly the right angle, it also had personality—Elaine May's—and there were two of her: as an actress playing an incredibly bumbling, bookish, absentminded botanist—a world-class klutz and eligible heiress who is numbingly shy—she was brilliant; as a vividly satirical writer and sharp-eyed director of comedy, she was immediately in full command. If this had been a drama, and someone had accomplished what Elaine did, the work would have been hailed to the skies; but comedy is always taken somewhat for granted, even though anyone who's ever done both will tell you comedy requires far greater skill and precision than drama. As Tallulah Bankhead put it: "An onion can make you cry, but show me the vegetable that can make you laugh!"

In that department, Walter Matthau is no slouch himself, and he has been giving vintage comedy performances
for years, being one of the last stars to come out of the studio system, though he hit his stride after its collapse. He is
also one of the last great personality actors—both a recog-
nizable personality and a superb actor.

In *A New Leaf*, as a pampered, insensitive, egotistical
playboy who suddenly finds himself flat broke, Matthau
does one of his most brilliant turns—hilariously insuffer-
able, pompous, vicious—as he disdainfully woos May's
pushover heiress, all the while plotting to murder her for
the fortune she innocently puts in his total control. She
even discovers a new species of fern, and instead of nam-
ing it (as is customary) after herself, she names it after
Matthau's character. He still plots right along to kill her.
Matthau is at the same time believably monstrous and still
terribly funny.

This is, therefore, perhaps the sunniest black comedy
ever made, but not as black as Ms. May would have had it.
Indeed, that became a major bone of contention between
Elaine and the studio: she wanted Matthau to kill a character (Jack Warden) to protect the heiress; the studio said that
was going too far. Elaine sued them and lost. That May's
character remains blissfully unaware of her lover's duplicity
only underscores the mordant darkness behind the comedy,
embodying two of the most dramatic sides of woman: the
character, profoundly innocent; the director-writer, deeply
knowing.

All of Elaine May's subsequent pictures featured equally
disenchanting male characters: Charles Grodin sees Cybill
Shepherd and drops bride Jeannie Berlin (Elaine's daughter)
on their honeymoon in *The Heartbreak Kid* (1972), most
cleverly written by Neil Simon (from a Bruce Jay Friedman
short story) and benefiting from probably the best direction

per se any screenplay of his has received. The two petty
hoodlums in May's *Mikey and Nicky* (1976), portrayed sublimely (and with lasting star allure) by John Cassavetes and
Peter Falk, constitute an uncompromisingly brutal, devastating look at a male friendship; one scene alone—when the
two visit a cemetery at night—is strikingly unique. May
again fought the studio on this, won the battle, but lost the
war. The picture is her cut; the studio buried the film. She
didn't direct again until *Ishtar* (1987), in which the two
guys have finally become complete idiots. Having Warren
Beatty and Dustin Hoffman do a kind of modern Abbott
and Costello is about as far as you could go. Long live
Elaine! Would that she could act and direct again in pictures. In 1998 I saw her perform off-Broadway in a couple
of one-act plays she wrote *(Power Plays)*, and her performances matched the comic genius of the writing.

OTHER ELAINE MAY PICTURES:
> *The Heartbreak Kid* (1972; with Charles Grodin, Cybill Shep-
> herd, Jeannie Berlin).
> *Mikey and Nicky* (1976; with Peter Falk, John Cassavetes).
> *Ishtar* (1987; with Warren Beatty, Dustin Hoffman).

THE CRIME OF MR. LANGE

Just about everyone knowledgeable seems to agree by now—nearly two decades since his death—that Jean Renoir, youngest son of the great Impressionist painter Auguste Renoir, and born September 15, 1894, was the best film director the Western world has known. (I'd vote for Kenji Mizoguchi as the Eastern world's finest; see Week 28). And one of Renoir's most defining, charm-filled, yet profoundly subversive works is *The Crime of Mr. Lange* (1936). The title in its original French—*Le Crime de Monsieur Lange*—contains a play on words that reveals part of the picture's thematic intention: In English, the *g* in *Lange* is hard, as in *sang*, but in French it is soft, as in *angel*, which in French is *l'ange*. So the French audience is prepared to see *The Crime of "Mr. Angel."*

This becomes all the more piquant when we realize—early on, because the bulk of the story plays in a long flashback framed by bar scenes—that the crime is a murder. The reluctant killer (René Lefèvre) turns out to be one of the kindest, most considerate, chivalrous, fair-dealing, innocent, and appealing young dreamers you could ever imagine. (And you may immediately recognize the deep influence this particular character had on François Truffaut's signature figure in a number of films, always personified by Jean-Pierre Léaud.) The other fugitive in the story is

Monsieur Lange's girlfriend (Odette Florelle), a coworker at the publishing house that Lange and others first worked for and then ran, with Lange himself supplying their most successful pulp serial, *The Adventures of Arizona Jim*—all Westerns written by Lange—though neither he nor anyone there has ever been to America. The man whom Lange kills is the owner of the publishing house, and is among the smarmiest, most insidious, politely vulgar, and strangely banal of heavies. And remember that at the time Renoir made this poetic comedy-drama of a justifiable homicide, Hitler and Mussolini were already in power.

One of the beautiful things about the picture is the keenly observed human microcosm created through the shared community of the publisher's offices. Superbly played by an ensemble called Le Groupe Octobre, the film was cowritten with the legendary French screenwriter and poet Jacques Prévert, most famous for his work in *Children of Paradise* (1945) and for the original French lyrics to that classic sad love song "Autumn Leaves." The picture is filled with seemingly simple, yet complicated, and remarkably fluid long takes—entire scenes played without cutting. Renoir pioneered these, starting in the early sound period, as a way of preserving the actor's total concentration and immersion in the role—as when the curtain's up on stage—but with the extreme mobility of the roaming camera eye.

Crime comes in the middle of Renoir's extraordinary second period, from his second talkie, *La Chienne* (1931), through *Boudu Saved from Drowning* (1932), *A Day in the Country* (1935), *Grand Illusion* (1937)—the first foreign-language film ever nominated for the best picture Oscar (see Week 16)—and *La Bête Humaine* (1938), and culminating with the sublime *The Rules of the Game* (see Week 48). After that film's initial failure, Renoir left France and eventually settled in Beverly Hills, whence he had a fascinating American period and a gloriously international final flowering. For me, Renoir provides in movies what Mozart provides in music: the ability to disturb and to heal both at once. His work also reminds those of us who really care about movies, and people, that no special effects or spectacle can ultimately match in emotion the sharp and honest revelation of human truths.

OTHER JEAN RENOIR PICTURES:

Le Chienne (1931; with Michel Simon).

Boudu Saved from Drowning (1932; with Michel Simon).

Toni (1934; with Charles Blavette, Max Dalban).

A Day in the Country (1935; with Sylvia Bataille, George Darnoux).

Also see Weeks 16 and 48.

MOGAMBO

John Ford always used to say that he tried to alternate his pictures by doing "one for them" and then "one for myself," meaning he would accept an assignment to satisfy the studios and the box office, and this would often enable him to get the backing for his more risky, personal projects. Ironically, sometimes the ones "for them" have endured as well as, if not better than, the others because of that intriguingly complicated tension between material and a director's way of handling it—an aspect of film that was among the most basic tenets of the French *politique des auteurs*, and is also one of the most difficult things to see in, and to convey about, a movie. *Mogambo* is a good example from Ford's work—and appropriate to this week's autumn equinox. This evocative, though largely forgotten, 1953 African love story stars Clark Gable, Ava Gardner, and Grace Kelly as the extremely potent sides of a triangle.

It was a remake: Gable himself had played the same role opposite Jean Harlow (doing Gardner's part) two decades earlier in one of his first big successes (also still a pretty fair picture), *Red Dust* (1932), directed by Victor Fleming. But Fleming was a competent though impersonal director, very dependent for quality on his script and cast, while Ford is among the precious few U.S. directors who could be termed a poet. Orson Welles called him "a poet and comedian," and both qualities are apparent in the gloriously color-photographed *Mogambo*. The uninspired title has no known meaning; legend has it the producer made up the name as a variant on his favorite nightclub, the Mocambo.

Gable plays an aging big-game hunter who basically makes his living by taking tourists on safaris. Kelly plays the repressed, frustrated, spoiled, and slightly hysterical wife of a pleasant young British anthropologist who hires Gable's services while Kelly yearns for his services in another capacity. Gardner plays a worldly wise showgirl who happens to get stranded at Gable's place and, after an antagonistic beginning, allows herself an affair with him, only to be humiliated when he takes up with Kelly. Ford's unusual treatment of all this is what gives the picture its distinction—that, combined with the three actors' excellent performances and their individual star personas. Gable lets himself be more unbuttoned than usual, more reckless, a consummate cocksman, often a heel. Kelly, in her last nonstarring role and her best work for anyone other than in the three Hitchcock pictures that followed, was nominated by the Academy for best supporting actress. The rumor is that she and Gable had an affair during the shooting, and their love scenes certainly don't disprove this. The wildly beautiful Ava Gardner, whom then-husband Frank Sinatra was visiting through some of the filming, was nominated as best actress for unquestionably her finest job in any movie; she's just brilliant in it.

Of course, Ford slants the film totally in Gardner's favor. Not only is she made the most sympathetic character but, in one sequence after another, things are subtly shown from her perspective, and she receives the most loving close-ups. Ford clearly adored her. In Gardner's first scene, the meeting between her and Gable, notice how Ford shoots her in the closer angle so that we are unconsciously seeing Gable from her point of view, and therefore identifying more with her than with him. This is typical of Ford's empathy with the underdog. Remember his treatment of Claire Trevor's "fallen woman" in *Stagecoach* (1939) or even Linda Darnell's misguided spitfire as she dies in *My Darling Clementine* (1946).

It was Ford's idea not to use a score for *Mogambo*, the only music being African tribal rhythms he recorded on location. His way of playing certain scenes without a cut or not going to a reaction shot when you most expect it, his expressive choice of where to put the camera and therefore the emphasis—all these give the work a personal intensity, a dynamic quite apart from the script or the actors—which used to be what film direction was all about. Speaking of influences in the movies, Howard Hawks once admitted to me, "It's hard to make a picture without thinking of Jack Ford." Just watching Ford do his thing in *Mogambo* becomes a valuable lesson in why Hawks said that.

OTHER JOHN FORD PICTURES:
    See Weeks 11, 22, and 50—and the recommendations that
        follow those films.

Claudette Colbert (right) leaves
her inventor-husband Joel
McCrea (left) in order to get
him money for his grand plans,
and she succeeds quite well by
meeting the richest man in
America, bespectacled Rudy
Vallee, and his man-eating
sister, Mary Astor, in Preston
Sturges's hilarious quadrille,
The Palm Beach Story (Week
40).
Photo courtesy The Kobal Collection.

OTHELLO

Toward the end of the Forties, after a tumultuous decade within the Hollywood studio system, Orson Welles went to Europe and began to prepare what would turn out to be the first modern independent film made by an American artist, and the first thoroughly cinematic picture based on a play by William Shakespeare: the striking, innovative 1952 Mercury production of *Othello*. To ensure complete independence, Welles acted in other people's movies (like *The Third Man* and *Prince of Foxes*) and used his salaries to pay for the shooting of his own film.

Because of his players' schedules and myriad other obstacles, the process took Welles nearly three years, but resulted in one of the most inspired and brilliant of his works and won him the grand prize at the 1952 Cannes Film Festival. Since he had shot a large part of the movie in Morocco, Welles submitted the film as a Moroccan entry. And so, as Orson loved to say, "The picture became the first [and probably only] Moroccan production to win a great international award!"

But the real nationality of the work is pure Welles via Shakespeare. Apart from Welles's own *Macbeth* (1948) and his Falstaff film, *Chimes at Midnight* (1966), his *Othello* is still the only artistically satisfying Shakespearean adaptation that is also truly a film, as opposed to photographed theater.

Since Verdi and his librettist Arrigo Boito had felt no compunction in altering the Bard's play when they created their grand opera *Otello*, Welles argued, why couldn't he be as free for this new medium? Tightening the tragedy from a usual three hours to a fast-paced ninety-one minutes, he begins with a funeral sequence for the suicide Othello, the Moor of Venice, and his murdered white wife Desdemona, then flashes back to the cause, starting dialogue with Iago's "I hate the Moor," sometimes replacing famous lines (like "I kissed thee ere I killed thee") with similarly memorable images that evoke the words, and proceeding with a kind of terrifying inevitability to the annihilating foregone conclusion.

When costumes didn't arrive in time, Welles decided to shoot a key night sequence—the murder of Roderigo—in a dark, steamy Turkish bath, thus requiring only towels. Welles's fearless inventiveness is evident throughout, giving the whole picture a remarkably fresh, spontaneous quality. Shot on numerous distant locations in Morocco and Italy, the film's black-and-white photography is sharply evocative, and Francesco Lavagnino's music has the classic size for epic tragedy. All the performances are excellent, but Micheál MacLiammóir's wily, quicksilver Iago stands out, as does Suzanne Cloutier's heartbreakingly innocent Desdemona. In the title role, Welles himself gives a subdued, extremely vulnerable reading of the proud, guileless man driven to insane jealousy, all because of one man's envy.

Orson understood those two super-deadly sins—the twins jealousy and envy—all too well, having been at the receiving end of them his entire creative life. After all, he had published revolutionary editions of Shakespeare's plays *(Everybody's Shakespeare)* while still a teenager, had scored on the New York stage with a voodoo *Macbeth* at twenty-one and a modern-dress *Julius Caesar* at twenty-two, and had directed, cowritten, produced, and starred in one of the greatest films ever made, *Citizen Kane* (see Week 18), at twenty-five. Certainly there was a lot of envy and jealousy that helped to prevent him from doing more work in pictures; he was simply too good not to be some kind of terrible rebuke to mediocrity. All this sort of thing similarly contributes to Iago's destruction of Othello.

But Welles survived. His *Othello*, though highly acclaimed all over Europe, was either ignored or despised by critics in his own country. Not until nearly a decade after Orson's death was *Othello* revived in the United States and finally hailed as the masterwork it had, of course, always been.

And for all those who ignorantly ask that tired old question, "What did Welles ever do after *Citizen Kane*?" the answer is, at the very least: *The Magnificent Ambersons* (see Week 26), *The Lady from Shanghai* (1948), and later that same year, *Macbeth*—his dark, rough sketch of Shakespeare's play, done in twenty-three days on old Western sets—*Othello*, *Mr. Arkadin* (1955), *Touch of Evil* (1958), *The Trial* (1963), and *Chimes at Midnight* (1966). He did more, too, but for God's sake, these alone put him at the very forefront of the world's greatest film artists. And as America's first independent, his example remains our brightest hope.

OTHER ORSON WELLES SHAKESPEARE-BASED PICTURES:
Macbeth (1948; with Welles, Dan O'Herlihy, Jeanette Nolan, Roddy McDowall).
Chimes at Midnight (1966; with Welles, John Gielgud, Keith Baxter, Jeanne Moreau, Margaret Rutherford).

THE PALM BEACH STORY

Preston Sturges's fifth-in-a-row success (see Weeks 2 and 10) was that wild 1942 satirical romantic comedy starring Claudette Colbert at her most scintillating, Joel McCrea, Mary Astor, and Rudy Vallee: *The Palm Beach Story.* This is the one where Colbert decides to leave her steadfast but struggling inventor-husband McCrea on the novel premise that an attractive woman can get a great deal more money on her own—in this case, for her husband's inventions—rather than *with* her husband around.

In rapid succession, while flat broke, she encounters the Weenie King, a small man with a wad that could choke a horse which he gladly peels off for her; the Ale and Quail Club, a drunken men's duck-shooting party that proceeds to make her their mascot and shoot up the train they're all on; and the richest man in America (Vallee's one immemorial movie turn), who falls head-over-heels in love with her. And all of that happens before they even *get* to Palm Beach.

Most appropriately, Sturges was the first person to win the original screenplay Oscar—for his first directing-writing job, 1940's sardonic *The Great McGinty*—though he used to write all his scripts by essentially acting them out for his secretary, who would take it all down in shorthand and type it up. Imagine the joy of being in *that* room! This unique improvising technique not only gives his dialogue remarkable freshness and immediacy, but makes it virtually actor-proof, especially since Sturges generally was writing his scripts with very specific actors in mind for each role; hence the famous Sturges Stock Company, with most of the same supporting actors in every picture. He could therefore improvise the words that would best fit these players.

After four popular and critical successes in two years, Sturges must have been much encouraged to let himself go, and *The Palm Beach Story* is perhaps his full-out wackiest comedy and his sunniest. The picture begins with a farcical chase sequence that is totally incomprehensible and never referred to until the very end of the movie, when it is re-called to mind in order to deliver the otherwise impossible happy ending. This, of course, is a terrific Sturges trade-mark: the unlikely triumph of happiness against all odds and all credulity. After all, it *is* a comedy.

Sturges had an unusually cosmopolitan upbringing—spending a great deal of time in France with his artistic mother, and receiving much love from his New York businessman father—and this mixture (as I touched on in Week 10) of sophisticated European objectivity with vividly American idiomatic energy creates a very special frisson not found in anyone else's work. (Something of the same combi-nation gives different but similarly memorable results in the American pictures of Ernst Lubitsch.) Toward the end of *The Palm Beach Story*, Rudy Vallee, a famous early crooner, serenades Colbert while she has a tryst with her estranged husband. This is a tart example of Sturges's mischievousness.

From Preston's short and miraculous golden moment when he could do no wrong, the film still carries with it an extraordinary certitude in its timing. An old-fashioned stance on Sturges is his supposed lack of visual grace. To me, he was a particularly splendid director of actors, who never distracted with his setups, indeed was always in the right place with his camera, and paced his sequences perfectly; most of all he respected the integrity of actors' performances and generally did long continuous takes to preserve this. As Orson Welles used to say, in talkies shooting like that was "what distinguished the men from the boys." In *The Palm Beach Story*, Sturges has a brilliant quartet of comic actors with some of his most insouciant dialogue. You may wonder, Where has this kind of America gone?

OTHER PRESTON STURGES PICTURES:
See Weeks 2 and 10—and the recommendations that follow those films.

CONTEMPT

While Brigitte Bardot was at the height of her international superstar fame and success—having been responsible through Roger Vadim's *And God Created Woman* in 1956 for breaking French cinema out of U.S. art houses and into the mainstream and thereby inadvertently also paving the way for the takeover in France of the New Wave filmmakers—she agreed to act in a movie by the most revolutionary of these *nouvelle vague* directors, Jean-Luc Godard, making his first (and pretty much only) "star picture." Adapted by Godard from Alberto Moravia's novel, *A Ghost at Noon,* the film costarred Jack Palance as a devious Hollywood producer, Michel Piccoli as Bardot's somewhat passive novelist-screenwriter husband, and legendary German pioneer Fritz Lang as a legendary German pioneer named Fritz Lang shooting for Palance an adaptation of Homer's *Odyssey.* With Godard appearing briefly as Lang's assistant director, the provocative color and wide-screen result opened in 1963 as *Contempt* (*Le Mépris* in French). For all these artists, the film stands among their finest hours.

In his quirky, idiosyncratic way, Godard achieves all his effects through an artful indirection, a circuitous-seeming but actually Spartan style that relies heavily on his actors' movements, gestures, body language, and intonation far more than words. Bardot is especially good at this—being a true-born movie-star personality as well as an increasingly resourceful actress—and this is one of her subtlest, most touching performances. What a world of joy and fulfillment Piccoli loses through his self-absorption, his ambition, his blindness to everything his loving Brigitte is signaling. It is the story of her contempt not only for Palance, with whom she will have an affair, but mainly for Piccoli, whom she eventually leaves. This is followed by a swift, shocking dénouement.

The film makes no moralizing statements, nor does it nudge you into complicity. Like Otto Preminger, whom he always admired, Godard presents all the facts—often only fleeting moments—and lets the audience decide what happened and why. *Contempt* is a cool, very troubling work, speaking directly to the most difficult war of all, the battle of the sexes, incisively revealing that central difference in how most men and most women think and feel.

The first shot in the picture presents Bardot lying naked on her stomach while talking with and listening to Piccoli: Godard's camera pans slowly over her body, giving the audience exactly what they thought they wanted but without preamble or foreplay, so that it is quite unsettling, overwhelming. Even here, with blatant nudity, Godard works through indirection. By handing us Bardot as we want her, he makes us uneasily question this very assumption; by getting this immediately out of the way, he allows us more easily to see Bardot through the rest of the story as considerably more than a naked body.

At one point, Piccoli—deceptively unmacho in a brilliantly subtle performance—puts on a cowboy hat and wears it in the bathtub; when Brigitte comments on this, Piccoli says he is emulating Dean Martin in *Some Came Running* (see Week 23). In that movie, Martin not only refuses to remove his cowboy hat, but also plays a largely unregenerate misogynist who only at the very end of the picture shows some respect and consideration for a woman: at Shirley MacLaine's funeral he finally takes off his hat. In *Contempt*, therefore, the cowboy hat is not simply a passing homage or inside joke from a cinema-hip director, but rather a revealing insight into this character's submerged lack of understanding of women. Fritz Lang's presence—a superbly shaded portrait of cynicism and sagacity, combined with an innate artistic conscience—is equally significant: the inescapability of fate was Lang's great theme. Godard here links fate irrevocably to character. Lang also brings a strong sense of aged wisdom, the only ray of hope in the entire piece. Now thirty-six years old, *Contempt* seems not only far more youthful, still modern, but in human relations still terribly relevant at the end of the 1990s.

OTHER JEAN-LUC GODARD PICTURES:
Breathless (1960; with Jean-Paul Belmondo, Jean Seberg).
A Woman Is a Woman (1961; with Jean-Paul Belmondo, Jean-Claude Brialy, Anna Karina).
Vivre Sa Vie/My Life to Live (1962; with Anna Karina).
Band of Outsiders (1964; with Anna Karina, Sami Frey, Claude Brasseur).
Alphaville (1965; with Eddie Constantine, Anna Karina, Akim Tamiroff).
Pierrot le Fou (1965; with Jean-Paul Belmondo, Anna Karina).
Masculine Feminine (1966; with Jean-Pierre Léaud).
Weekend (1968; with Mireille Darc, Jean Yanne, Jean-Pierre Léaud).

TWENTIETH CENTURY

If you want to see Drew Barrymore's grandfather, the legendary Great Profile and world-class star actor John Barrymore, in his best movie performance—he himself was quoted as saying "I've never done anything I like as well . . . a role that comes once in an actor's lifetime"—do not miss Howard Hawks's hilarious trend-setting show-business comedy, *Twentieth Century.* This 1934 breakneck screwball farce, costarring the glorious Carole Lombard, was scripted by the brilliant team of Ben Hecht and Charles MacArthur.

Though Barrymore is generally remembered as a great tragedian, a memorable romantic presence on stage and screen, his earliest successes on Broadway in the Twenties were all as a superb light comic player, a matinee idol, too, but in "Tennis anyone?" drawing-room comedies. Indeed, Barrymore himself—who preferred painting to acting but was forced by family tradition into theater—always enjoyed doing comedy more.

His tour de force here as a manipulative, egomaniacal Broadway producer-director-showman-charlatan (supposedly inspired by Jed Harris, who had helped make Hecht-MacArthur's *The Front Page* a smashing success) is extraordinarily layered, comically complicated, absolutely outrageous, and yet totally believable—certainly to us theatrical folks.

Orson Welles used to say that when doing comedy neither he nor Laurence Olivier could ever get over Barrymore's performance of Oscar Jaffe in *Twentieth Century*, and that in some way they were still doing Barrymore in that movie. Virtually every single moment of Barrymore's work here is priceless, and many of these moments are unforgettable—the way he leaps in the air in the posture of an archer as he cries "Sagittarius!" or imitates a camel while doing a pitch, or the way he meditatively, then triumphantly, picks his nose—shot by Hawks, of course, at the profile, for which Jack (to his friends) Barrymore was justly famous.

Right up there with him in comic genius—and a knockout in her own right—is the wondrous and unique Ms. Lombard, for whom the term for the movie genre "screwball" was coined a couple of years later when she did the screwiest society girl ever seen, opposite her ex-husband William Powell in Gregory La Cava's memorable and still delectable Depression-era comedy, *My Man Godfrey* (1936). Having been discovered by Allan Dwan playing ball on the streets as a twelve-year-old tomboy, Lombard did some silent knockabout comedies, yet had been acting very straight roles in movies since the talkies started. But, Hawks told me, he had seen her at a Hollywood party "with a couple of drinks in her" and thought "she was hilarious and uninhibited," so he cast her in *Twentieth Century* in the challenging role of shop girl Mildred Plotka, whom Barrymore's Jaffe molds Svengali-like into theatrical star Lilly Garland, seducing her at the same time.

Jaffe's insane jealousy and manipulativeness eventually drive her away to Hollywood and picture stardom, while without Garland, his fortunes hit rock bottom. He runs into her again by accident on the Twentieth Century Limited—the famous deluxe train that used to run between New York and Chicago—whence came the title's direct meaning, the filmmakers also fully conscious of its allusion to our crazy age. And for the rest of the picture, he plots to get her back again on his stage and in his bed.

When shooting started, Lombard was so nervous, according to Hawks, that "she was emoting all over the place . . . trying very hard and . . . was just dreadful." Hawks broke for lunch early and took Carole for a walk to loosen her up. What would she do, he asked, if someone insulted her in a certain way? She replied, "I'd kick him in the balls." Hawks said that since Barrymore was insulting her that way, why didn't she kick *him*? And so, in the first scene they shot—which comes sometime in the middle of the picture—Lombard leans way back on her seat and tries repeatedly to kick Barrymore while he's yelling at her. As soon as the shot was finished, Barrymore yelled out, "That was fabulous!"

This filmed moment at the birth of a great comedienne is only one of many exhilaratingly funny exchanges between Barrymore and Lombard, a show-biz relationship defined and elaborated as never before—too hip for the room, as it turned out, the picture being only a marginal success in its day. Even now, there remains an inside quality to it that plays best to show people who know its many exaggerations aren't really much exaggerated. The picture also marks the first use in movies of rapid, overlapping dialogue, written under Hawks's supervision so that it could be accomplished without actually losing any of the important words. This had profound reverberations in the business, as did Hawks's getting the male and female leads to do the sort of physical humor—like the kicking—previously reserved only for the comedy relief. Frank Capra did a touch of this, but to a much lesser degree, the same year in his Oscar-sweeping *It Happened One Night*. Of course, Noël Coward—whom Hawks much admired—had done it first on the stage four years earlier with Gertrude Lawrence in his own *Private Lives*, filmed with a different cast and little success at MGM in 1931.

OTHER HOWARD HAWKS COMEDIES:
See Week 29—and the recommendations that follow that film.
See also Weeks 4 and 24—and the recommendations following those films.

GLORIA

In 1980, John Cassavetes wrote and directed, and Columbia Pictures released, an explosive movie John had done everything he could to avoid making, including asking me to direct it instead. Cassavetes, remember, was the brilliantly iconoclastic actor-filmmaker who, more than anyone except Orson Welles, had essentially inaugurated America's independent film movement with his groundbreaking series of realistic, yet strangely stylized, slices of life such as *Shadows* (1961), *Faces* (1968), *Husbands* (1970), *Minnie and Moskowitz* (1971), and *A Woman Under the Influence* (1974).

He wrote a script, first called *One Winter Night*, in which an entire Spanish-American family, except for one little boy, is wiped out in a mob hit, and an ex–gun moll reluctantly finds herself saving the kid as the killers go after him. But Cassavetes felt the basically melodramatic thriller material wasn't really his thing, that he had written the script to make some money by selling it, not by making it himself. When he came after me to do it, besides feeling flattered, I said he was the only one who could make its complicated dualities work. Eventually, not very happily, he gave in and agreed to shoot the picture himself if he could use his wife and frequent collaborator, the uniquely talented and beautiful Gena Rowlands. Columbia said he could, but only if

Barbra Streisand wouldn't do it. Barbra was still annoyed at John for turning down her offer for him to direct the rock 'n' roll *A Star Is Born* (1976) and also justly felt no one would believe her as a mob doll; so she passed, Gena was cast, and, fortunately, John made one of his most financially successful and expressively subversive works, finally titled *Gloria.*

Sometime after Cassavetes' tragic death in 1989, shortly before his sixtieth birthday, Gena would tell me that the main reason John didn't want to do the movie was the terrible massacre of that whole family, which sets the picture's story in motion. But one of the things that makes the film so effective is precisely this tension between Cassavetes' poetic temperament and the devastatingly violent material he was treating. Ultimately, the picture is one of a kind in the way it turns upside down everything the normal gangster shoot-'em-up does. That an attractive woman is the strongest yet most deeply compassionate figure in the whole piece—a kind of feminine variation on John Wayne, Humphrey Bogart, and James Cagney—is what gives the work its extraordinary resonance and distinction. It might well have been adopted as a centerpiece for feminism: in a cold and out-of-control universe, an increasingly urban jungle without rules or honor, the woman as archetype of both destruction and salvation is certainly a valid statement.

And no one could have portrayed this better than Gena Rowlands, among America's finest actresses. Her Gloria and her Woman *(. . . Under the Influence)* are the quintessential two sides—strong and broken—of the modern female psyche. Cassavetes' *Gloria* presents a New York City you've never seen quite like this: ominous, dangerous, unpredictable, a microcosm of the world at large. The little boy, played by John Adames, also gives a superb performance; director-actor Vittorio De Sica *(Bicycle Thief, Shoeshine)* once said you're not a director until you've directed a child. Cassavetes certainly was a director like no other, and contrary to popular conception he also (except for *Shadows*, which *was* improvised) *wrote* all his own scripts. John was our most revolutionary filmmaker, whose restless and uncompromising vision remains vividly contemporary, challenging, provocative, and at its heart darkly lyrical. If there was ever an American Jean Renoir, Cassavetes was the one.

OTHER JOHN CASSAVETES–GENA ROWLANDS PICTURES:

A Child Is Waiting (1963; with Judy Garland, Burt Lancaster).

Faces (1968; with John Marley, Lynn Carlin, Seymour Cassel).

Minnie and Moskowitz (1971; with Seymour Cassel).

A Woman Under the Influence (1974; with Peter Falk).

Opening Night (1977; with Cassavetes, Ben Gazzara, Joan Blondell).

Love Streams (1984; with Cassavetes).

OTHER CASSAVETES PICTURES:

Shadows (1961; with Lelia Goldoni, Ben Carruthers, Tony Ray).

Too Late Blues (1962; with Bobby Darin, Stella Stevens).

Husbands (1970; with Cassavetes, Peter Falk, Ben Gazzara).

The Killing of a Chinese Bookie (1976; with Ben Gazzara).

"I'll never forget the weekend Laura died . . ." is the start of Otto Preminger's haunting thriller, *Laura* (Week 46). Dana Andrews is the tough cop brought in to solve the case, falling for the dead woman's portrait, and is shocked (and a touch disappointed?) when the real Laura—in the person of Gene Tierney—turns up wondering what he's doing in her living room.

Photo courtesy Photofest.

INVASION OF
THE BODY SNATCHERS

Something chilling for Halloween . . .

The most haunting, strangely prophetic science-fiction picture ever made has the worst pulp title—which all the creative people hated, and which the studio imposed, along with the dreaded prologue and epilogue—Don Siegel's 1956 masterpiece of understated terror: *Invasion of the Body Snatchers*. Siegel and veteran producer Walter Wanger wanted to name it with a quote from Shakespeare's *Hamlet: Sleep No More*. Adapted from a Jack Finney novel, by Daniel Mainwaring and Siegel—Clint Eastwood's favorite director (five films including 1971's *Dirty Harry*)—the spookily metaphoric plot deals with a small-town doctor who slowly comes to realize that several patients and friends are being taken over by some sort of human-duplicating alien pods in such a way that they all end up looking exactly like the real people but lack any true emotion.

The film was made just as the McCarthy era ended, and its references to that sort of mass hysteria are unmistakable. But director Siegel (one of the studio system's undercover mavericks) and producer Wanger (never a team player, either, and a New York sophisticate) had broader issues in mind on this B-budget movie which no one took very seriously on its release. As Siegel told me in the late Sixties, ". . . I felt that this was a very important story. I think the world is populated by pods and I wanted to show them. . . . So many people have no feeling about cultural things, no feeling of pain, of sorrow." The studio heads of the long-defunct Allied Artists, whom Siegel characterized as pods, were afraid of the unmitigated horror of the original ending, in which Kevin McCarthy (exceptional as the doctor) has fled his small town, is lost on a freeway where he sees numerous trucks filled with pods heading into the heart of the country, and screams directly to the audience: "They're coming! You're next!" So Siegel and Wanger were forced to put the whole picture in the form of a flashback which, among other things, tends to destroy suspense since you know the doctor has survived to tell the tale. Running this film without the prologue and consequent epilogue, as Siegel said, "would be a lot closer to the way" the film was conceived.

The utter sense of everyday reality is what makes this work so effective and memorable, a triumph of talent over financial limitations, therefore of truly imaginative direction. I remember an underground New York screening in the late Fifties with Ray Bradbury in attendance, before this film had become the noted cult picture it is today; I believe it's one of Ray's favorites and there isn't a better authority on the genre. The transformation of Dana Wynter at the end is one of the most subtly terrifying moments in picture history.

OTHER DON SIEGEL PICTURES:
   The Verdict (1946; with Sydney Greenstreet, Peter Lorre).
   The Big Steal (1949; with Robert Mitchum, Jane Greer).
   Riot in Cell Block 11 (1954; with Neville Brand).
   Crime in the Streets (1956; with John Cassavetes, Sal Mineo).
   Baby Face Nelson (1957; with Mickey Rooney, Carolyn Jones, Sir Cedric Hardwicke).

The Lineup (1958; with Eli Wallach).
Hell Is for Heroes (1962; with Steve McQueen).
The Killers (1964; with Lee Marvin, John Cassavetes, Angie Dickinson, Ronald Reagan).
Madigan (1968; with Richard Widmark, Henry Fonda).
Coogan's Bluff (1968; with Clint Eastwood).
Dirty Harry (1971; with Clint Eastwood).
The Shootist (1976; with John Wayne, Lauren Bacall).
Escape from Alcatraz (1979; with Clint Eastwood).

ARSENIC AND OLD LACE

The lawyers for Dr. Jack Kevorkian might consider screening for the jury the only euthanasia picture I can think of, that comedy about two adorable little old ladies in Brooklyn who took pity on a score of lonely aged men with no families, gave them elderberry wine spiked with arsenic, and buried them with a nice Christian service in their cellar. Joseph Kesselring's smash Broadway farce was filmed in 1941 by none other than Frank Capra; it featured the two brilliant actresses who had originated their parts on the stage—wondrous Josephine Hull and dear Jean Adair— and starred Cary Grant as their nephew.

The rights contract, however, stipulated that the movie couldn't open until the New York run ended, and so the release had to be delayed until 1944, at which point *Arsenic and Old Lace* became an immediate picture classic. Indeed, the film holds up better than some of Capra's other, more typical work—like the fondly remembered *Mr. Deeds Goes to Town* (1936) or the Oscar-winning (for best picture) *You Can't Take It with You* (1938)—and was in its time one of Capra's last popular achievements.

Grant himself never spoke fondly of the picture— mainly, he used to say he'd given his entire salary to "the war effort"—and felt his performance was over the top. It is, but I'm fond of it, anyway, since it's very appropriate to the general wildness of the piece. The two ladies' brother, after all, thinks he's Teddy Roosevelt, and every time he climbs the stairs, he does it as though he's charging up San Juan Hill.

Another long-absent relative who drops by is a bizarre serial torturer-killer, originated on the stage by Boris Karloff in semi-Frankenstein-monster makeup. When someone asks for a description of this character, they're told he looks like Boris Karloff. Unfortunately, Karloff was stuck on Broadway and couldn't do the movie, and so Raymond Massey is made up to look like him, and is properly chilling. His weird sidekick is a bogus doctor of sorts, done to perfection by the superbly witty Peter Lorre. Anyway, in this sort of black-farce company, Grant's hysteria is certainly not out of key; when he first finds a dead body hidden in his aunts' window seat, his seven-take reaction of disbelief is absolutely brilliant and, in context, totally believable.

In fact, the movie's mood fits quite well with today's usual ultradark humor, yet is never depressing or disgusting. Because the script makes absolutely no pretense toward Capraesque social consciousness, there is a likably breezy tone to the direction, as though Capra was taking a vacation from weightiness and enjoying it very much. After all, he did begin in silent pictures as a gag writer and comedy director, making two excellent Harry Langdon pictures, *The Strong Man* (1926) and *Long Pants* (1927), and winning his first Oscar for the vintage screwball romantic comedy *It Happened One Night* (1934). The challenge of *Arsenic and Old Lace* was to take a remarkably successful stage play and make it work as well on the screen. He does.

The top-notch supporting cast includes Priscilla Lane as the happily normal (and insistently nubile) girl next door who Grant has just married but can't take on their honeymoon because of the continuing family crises: a good running gag is the cab Grant keeps waiting throughout the entire picture. Jack Carson is the pushy neighborhood cop who has written a play that he keeps wanting to pitch to Grant—who is a famous drama critic—and finally ties him to a chair to get his full attention. Even Edward Everett Horton makes a delightful appearance as the head of the funny farm to which Grant intends to send his loving but out-of-control relatives. Kids being more ghoulish these days than ever, *Arsenic and Old Lace* is probably as good a holiday treat as you can find for them among the treasures of the past.

OTHER FRANK CAPRA COMEDIES:
  The Strong Man (1926; with Harry Langdon).
  Long Pants (1927; with Harry Langdon).
  Platinum Blonde (1931; with Jean Harlow).
  Lady for a Day (1933; with May Robson, Warren William).
  It Happened One Night (1934; with Clark Gable, Claudette Colbert).
  Broadway Bill (1934; with Warner Baxter, Myrna Loy).
  You Can't Take It with You (1938; with Jean Arthur, Lionel Barrymore, James Stewart).
  A Hole in the Head (1959; with Frank Sinatra).

Also see Week 27.

LAURA

The one picture Otto Preminger directed which virtually everyone—even diehard anti-Premingerists—have always agreed was brilliant is his 1944 romantic murder mystery–suspense classic *Laura*. The movie is set among trendy Manhattanites, and its exceptional screenplay evolved from a clever twist in a Vera Caspary novel.

Though Preminger as producer had developed the material, 20th Century-Fox's studio head, Darryl Zanuck, had been infuriated by Preminger on another movie (Otto had only directed four passable programmers) and was not allowing him to direct, instead hiring veteran Rouben Mamoulian. Yet Preminger as producer persisted and prevailed in all casting decisions, including the use of Broadway star Clifton Webb, whose first film this became. But neither Preminger nor Zanuck liked Mamoulian's footage, and eventually the director was fired and Preminger allowed to take over.

The unusual movie still did not go easily and almost got recut and dumped, until legendary New York newspaper columnist Walter Winchell saw it at a private Zanuck screening and told the studio chief that it was a terrific, sophisticated East Coast job that the public would like. Winchell proved correct, and the success of *Laura* assured Preminger's directing-producing career, which resulted in at least three other masterworks: *Anatomy of a Murder* (1959), *Exodus* (1960), and *Advise and Consent* (1962).

Exceedingly ambiguous, *Laura* has the modern advantage of continually surprising the viewer with the twists and turns of the various characters, none of them predictable. The cold, acerbic newspaper columnist (Webb at his best) is madly in love; the beautiful murdered career girl (Gene Tierney in one of her loveliest performances) turns out to be anything but what she seems to the tough no-nonsense cop investigating the homicide (a defining role for Dana Andrews), a cop who finds it easier to fall for a dead woman than a live one. The film has an opening line—Webb's voice: "I'll never forget the weekend Laura died. . . ."—as memorable as its closing quote from an Ernest Dowson poem—Webb's voice again: "They are not long, the days of wine and roses. . . ." But since you may not have seen the film, I don't want to spoil it by explaining how these two moments also turn out to be by no means what they seem.

The famous musical score was done by newcomer David Raksin, dominated of course by Laura's theme, which, when lyrics were later added (after the film's release) by Johnny Mercer ("Laura is the face in the misty light / Footsteps that you hear down the hall. . . .") became a pop and jazz standard. In the plot, the tune is an instrumental record Laura used to play over and over; Vincent Price (in a superb performance) refers to it condescendingly: "Not exactly classical—but sweet . . ." That sort of hip self-awareness informs the whole piece—Webb responds to a question about his using a fountain pen: "No, I write with a goose quill dipped in venom"—and vividly shows the sort of good influence New York used to have on Hollywood.

Laura reveals Preminger's sharp intellect, good taste, wit, sense of craft, ease of delivery, incisiveness, and economy. Otto was a pro, and one of the finest and most influential filmmakers of the Forties into the Seventies who almost single-handedly broke down the walls of movie censorship and blacklisting. To the end, he believed firmly in what he called "the intelligence of the audience."

OTHER OTTO PREMINGER–GENE TIERNEY PICTURES:
   Whirlpool (1950; with José Ferrer).
   Where the Sidewalk Ends (1950; with Dana Andrews).
   Advise and Consent (1962; with Henry Fonda, Charles Laughton, Walter Pidgeon).

OTHER PREMINGER SUSPENSE PICTURES:
   Angel Face (1953; with Jean Simmons, Robert Mitchum).
   Bunny Lake Is Missing (1965; with Laurence Olivier, Carol Lynley, Keir Dullea, Noël Coward).

Also see Week 5.

THE CROWD

Back in 1962, upon first seeing King Vidor's extraordinary 1928 masterwork of complex simplicity, *The Crowd,* when the movie was already thirty-four years old, I noted how modern it seemed. I recently saw the picture again; now it's more than seventy years old, and it seems more modern than ever. Maybe this is because human nature and "regular average people"—which is what the film is about—don't really change very much and therefore their stories don't date. (Thus a good choice for Thanksgiving.) And the quality of the direction, photography, and acting is so high that, seeing the film on the big screen again after thirty-six years, I remembered image after image as though I had just seen it a month before.

Watching *The Crowd* this time—with those two breathtakingly real performances by Eleanor Boardman (who was also still Mrs. King Vidor at the time) and then-unknown James Murray—I also felt a kind of shock of recognition: Yes, this is how moving pictures used to be made, hardly a line of dialogue really necessary, with a remarkable economy of means and gesture, and a universality within the very particular specifics that has the ease and depth of a Mozart symphony. In the final, and perhaps greatest, year of the silent screen, *The Crowd* stands at the summit with such others of that year's many enduring glories as Erich von Stroheim's

The Wedding March or Josef von Sternberg's *Docks of New York*. But *The Crowd* is the most profoundly moving.

Though it deals only with a fairly typical American couple out of the crowd—their meeting, courtship, marriage, children, hopes, tragic losses—the film effortlessly achieves an amazing mythic size: Everyman and Everywoman at the end of the 1920s, and yet forever, Everywhere. This aspect is achieved entirely through Vidor's bold and vivid choice of camera angle—his compositional skills are striking. Note the stylized evocation of both objective and subjective reality on the death of the boy's father all in one fixed staircase shot. Having a complete mastery not only of the sustained shot but of montage as well, Vidor also had an obviously potent rapport with his actors.

King Wallis Vidor (1894–1982) had started in pictures as a newsreel cameraman. Showing his unique view immediately, he directed his first feature in 1919, and created in 1925 one of the most popular and highly acclaimed pictures in silent film history and probably the finest American World War I drama, *The Big Parade,* which made John Gilbert the top male star at MGM. The following year, Lillian Gish, then the reigning queen at MGM, chose Vidor to direct her as the ill-fated Mimi in their highly successful and extremely touching version of *La Bohème.* These hits gave Vidor the clout to make whatever he wanted next, and to do it entirely his way.

The result was *The Crowd,* and although it is, unquestionably, Vidor's most lasting silent achievement (despite its lack of popularity at the time), it must also be counted high among the artistically most important and influential U.S. films. The work predates in approach, and points the way for, such more-often-cited examples of "realistic street cinema" as Jean Renoir's *Toni* (1935) in France or the entire Italian neorealist movement led by Roberto Rossellini,

Vittorio De Sica, and others, 1945–1949. Several of Vidor's riveting images and evocative shots made their way through the years into numerous imitations or homages, such as Billy Wilder's blatant tip-of-the-hat, in his 1960 Oscar-winner *The Apartment*, to the great sea-of-desks shot.

The Crowd is an astonishingly powerful emotional experience, and although its ending is extremely ambiguous, the picture is not depressing for a moment. My dear mother always used to say that "a good work of art is never depressing. Sad, yes, but not depressing." Indeed, Vidor's *The Crowd* is strangely uplifting because of the resilience it shows in human nature, in this case especially the woman's nature, which manages to keep the man going after he has reached his lowest ebb. The final shot of the family of three laughing at a movie comedy in a darkened theater as the camera pulls away so far that they disappear back into "the crowd" is one of the great Pirandelloesque moments in cinema, for we too suddenly become a part of *The Crowd*, another audience in another theater but all basically the same.

If you want a pointed reminder that these days, as Hitchcock already observed in the late Sixties, "most films are simply pictures of people talking" (or, today, of things being blown up), see how the director here uses images alone not only to tell the story, but to express the deepest feelings of the characters and the largest possible application of these to life. King Vidor was a lovely man, reticent but passionately dedicated, wise and unpretentious, kind and encouraging; to the end, he adored the picture medium he had helped to create, and knew its (still) untold possibilities.

The Crowd is one of the very few uncompromising works of humanist art in world cinema.

OTHER KING VIDOR PICTURES:

The Big Parade (1925; with John Gilbert, Renée Adorée).

La Bohème (1926; with Lillian Gish, John Gilbert).

Show People (1928; with Marion Davies, William Haines).

Hallelujah! (1929; Nina Mae McKinney, Daniel Haynes).

Street Scene (1931; with Sylvia Sidney, William Collier Jr.).

The Champ (1931; with Wallace Beery, Jackie Cooper).

Our Daily Bread (1934; with Tom Keene, Karen Morley).

Stella Dallas (1937; with Barbara Stanwyck, Alan Hale Sr.).

The Citadel (1938; with Robert Donat, Rosalind Russell).

Northwest Passage (1940; with Spencer Tracy, Robert Young).

Duel in the Sun (1947; with Jennifer Jones, Gregory Peck).

The Fountainhead (1949; with Gary Cooper, Patricia Neal).

Ruby Gentry (1952; with Jennifer Jones, Charlton Heston).

Margaret Sullavan and James Stewart (right) are two employees at Matuscheck's department store in Budapest who do not get along, unaware that they are secret pen pals of great affinity in Ernst Lubitsch's wonderful human comedy, *The Shop Around the Corner* (Week 52); with the superb Felix Bressart as their long-suffering coworker.
Photo courtesy Photofest.

THE RULES
OF THE GAME

Among the five best films ever made is Jean Renoir's 1939 tragic romantic comedy, *The Rules of the Game (La Règle du Jeu)*, which in its original French release was so despised by press and public that some members of the opening-night audience pulled out seats and threw them at the screen. The original 113 minutes were trimmed to 100 minutes, and then to 80 minutes, yet still the picture was barely seen. Renoir fled in fury and heartbreak to the United States—specifically to Beverly Hills—where he was resident the rest of his life; though he returned to work in France in the Fifties and Sixties, he never lived there again.

The film lay forgotten until the Fifties, when it was discovered by the French New Wave filmmakers and critics, and subsequently restored by them in 1959 to its original version with only one minute lost. This premiered to great acclaim at the Venice Film Festival, and since then, *The Rules of the Game* has become an acknowledged work of genius, taste, visionary perception, tragic size. In a 1962 international poll of critics, the film was picked as the third greatest of all time. It is, indeed, as airy and weighty, as filled with light and shadows, as the shimmering Mozart music that opens it.

An extraordinarily prescient look at upper-middle-class society on the brink of World War II—the pettiness, self-obsession, hypocrisy, infidelities, mind games, frivo-lousness—it contains probably the single greatest line in pictures. In rough translation: "The only terrible thing in life is that everyone has their own good reasons." And the line is thrown away in long shot, spoken by Renoir, the director himself playing an artist—the saintly, benevolent, conciliatory artist—who nevertheless sets in motion the series of events that culminates in a hero's death. The essentially casual, underplayed, lightly paced manner, with even some dark physical comedy, belies the profoundly serious nature of the piece, vivified by an indelible sequence of savage bird and rabbit slaughter.

Yet all this is a reflection not only of the approaching catastrophe of 1939–1945, but also of the brutality of class relations during a weekend party at the mansion of a wealthy and adulterous young couple, surrounded by sycophants and lovers, superbly played by Renoir, Marcel Dalio (memorable from Renoir's *Grand Illusion*—see Week 16), Nora Gregor, Roland Toutain, Paulette Dubost, Gaston Modot, Mila Parély, and Julien Carette. Many of the sequences contain long continuous shots of remarkable complexity that never call attention to themselves but rather increase the sense of truth and the intensity of the actors' performances. It is a technique Renoir pioneered in the early talkies and which he here brings to the deepest fruition.

I was fortunate enough to have known Renoir (see Weeks 16 and 37) over the last fifteen years of his life and can say unequivocally that no other artist I have met approached his humanity or poetic vision. In trying to find the words to describe him, I'm reminded of a poem quoted by Robert Graves (in *The White Goddess*) as "a summary of the ideal poetic temperament"; the second Lord Falkland wrote the lines in tribute to that greatest of Elizabethans,

Ben Jonson, but they apply perfectly to the Jean Renoir I knew.

> *He had an infant's innocence and truth,*
> *The judgment of gray hairs, the wit of youth,*
> *Not a young rashness, not an ag'd despair,*
> *The courage of the one, the other's care;*
> *And both of them might wonder to discern,*
> *His ableness to teach, his skill to learn.*

That *The Rules of the Game*, a still amazingly relevant masterwork, was so violently misunderstood in its native country in its own day only proves that the United States doesn't have a monopoly on shortsightedness.

OTHER JEAN RENOIR PICTURES:
Swamp Water (1941; with Walter Huston, Anne Baxter, Walter Brennan).
The Southerner (1945; with Zachary Scott, Betty Field).
The River (1951; with Nora Swinburne, Arthur Shields).
The Golden Coach (1953; with Anna Magnani).
Elena and Her Men (1956; with Ingrid Bergman, Mel Ferrer, Jean Marais).
Le Petit Théâtre de Jean Renoir (1969; with Renoir, Jeanne Moreau).

Also see Weeks 16 and 37.

THE MERRY WIDOW

In the first year of full sound (1929), it was Ernst Lubitsch (see Weeks 12 and 52) who made the first all-talking, all-singing, all-dancing musical comedy, the delightful *The Love Parade*, starring Maurice Chevalier (in his first American feature) and Jeanette MacDonald (in her sexy, pre–Nelson Eddy period). Over the next four years, Lubitsch made four more romantic-comedy musicals, the last of which was the best of all (though the least popular at the time), his thoroughly divine 1934 version of Franz Lehár's famous operetta, *The Merry Widow*. It's Chevalier and MacDonald for the final intoxicating time, both of them again from another typically Lubitsch Ruritanian country, she the richest woman in the land, he a soldier of the king charged to use his charms to lure her back home after she runs off to Paris.

Witty, often hilarious, sometimes bittersweet, but always effervescent, the picture is also perhaps Lubitsch's most pointed look at cocksmanship: "Here they are," Jeanette tells Maurice at the (thinly disguised) bordello, where he is surrounded by adoring courtesans, "all your little tonights—and not a tomorrow among them." Later—in an ironically intended reversal of his real feelings and because he is so miserable at having been misjudged (by his peers) and misunderstood (by MacDonald, the widow he now adores)—

Chevalier declares at his trial: "Any man who can dance through life with hundreds of women, and chooses to walk through life with one, should be . . . hanged!" But later still, when MacDonald makes him repeat this mantra, he changes the last word to: ". . . married!"

While a film with a similar plot, and the same title, was made in 1925 by Erich von Stroheim as a harshly realistic black comedy of royal bad manners, Lubitsch completely transforms the dated operetta with a beautifully constructed, somewhat risqué, and ruefully wise scenario, cowritten by his frequent collaborator, the brilliant Samson Raphaelson (see Week 12). Chevalier, having tried and failed to seduce the fabulously wealthy widow, is ordered by the king (a wonderfully anachronistic performance by George Barbier) to make her fall for him and then bring her back from Paris to their country, which is dangerously diminished economically. Unhappy with the assignment, Maurice goes to Maxim's—where, as the song goes, "all the girls are dreams"—and there meets one Fifi who, unbeknownst to him (because he has only seen her in a mask of mourning), is the widow herself. She's gone there hoping to run into *him*! The trouble is he falls for Fifi—hook, line, and sinker—and she for him. Imagine their surprise at the embassy ball when they are introduced to each other as their real selves by the Ruritanian ambassador (a typical elegantly funny turn by the incomparable Edward Everett Horton). Naturally, just when Chevalier is about to explain the ridiculous but lovely situation to MacDonald, the ambassador screws things up by inadvertently blowing the whistle on Chevalier's royally ordered mission. Now disillusioned, Jeanette spurns Maurice. Hence the trial.

The score—with lyrics cleverly updated and music lushly orchestrated by none other than Lorenz Hart and Richard Rodgers—is one of the best for any musical, featuring such favorites as "I'm Going to Maxim's," "Girls, Girls, Girls," the haunting, bewitching "Vilia, Witch of the Wood," plus, naturally, the justly immortal "Merry Widow Waltz," danced beautifully by a terrific embassy-full of couples. And there is an amazing seduction scene that contains one of the most glorious camera moves in picture history: as first Jeanette alone, and then Maurice with her, dance "The Merry Widow Waltz," Lubitsch's camera somehow waltzing with them.

Featured among the supporting players is Hermann Bing, brother of the late lamented impresario of New York's Metropolitan Opera, Rudolph Bing. In an outrageously funny sequence with Horton, Bing does probably the greatest comic-German turn in movies. Horton has received from his king a mystifying coded missive that begins with the phrase "Lilac time," so he instructs Bing to look this up in the Ruritanian code book, and Bing, with the most delicate aplomb, reads (in a heavy accent) the translation: "You are the greatest idiot in the whole diplomatic service!" This is only the beginning of a golden few minutes, Hermann Bing's passport to film immortality. A victim of an anti-German Hollywood blacklist caused by the Hitler years, Bing (who also appears in Week 42's *Twentieth Century*) eventually committed suicide. This "Lilac time" sequence shows what a genius of comedy was lost.

I try to see Lubitsch's *The Merry Widow* at least once a year, and it has never let me down. On the contrary, it ranks high among my most favorite movies. I showed it to my daughters before they were ten and they still, twenty years later, love it as much as I do, and we all quote from it as a family tradition.

OTHER ERNST LUBITSCH–MAURICE CHEVALIER–JEANETTE
MacDONALD MUSICALS:
   The Love Parade (1929; with Lupino Lane, Lillian Roth).
   One Hour with You (1932; with Charlie Ruggles, Roland
   Young).

ANOTHER LUBITSCH-CHEVALIER MUSICAL:
   The Smiling Lieutenant (1931; with Claudette Colbert,
   Miriam Hopkins).

ANOTHER LUBITSCH-MacDONALD MUSICAL:
   Monte Carlo (1930; with Jack Buchanan, Zasu Pitts).

Also see Weeks 12 and 52.

HOW GREEN WAS MY VALLEY

The 1941 Academy Awards are often denigrated because Orson Welles's maverick *Citizen Kane* didn't win best picture that year. Usually overlooked, therefore, is the movie that did win—one of the finest classic American films, though it's about a Welsh coal-mining family: John Ford's profoundly touching visualization of Richard Llewellyn's best-selling novel, *How Green Was My Valley*. Coincidentally, both *Kane* and *How Green* are about the dissolution of family, but while *Kane*, in a modern way, seems to throw that part of the story away until the end, it is the essential plot of *How Green*. Both films were also made with the war in Europe about to expand into World War II, and the impermanence of the time is reflected in these two stories of impermanence and loss.

It was Ford's last commercial film for five years—all those spent on active duty in the Navy and with the Office of Strategic Services—and, because it is so personal to Ford and so typical of his main themes (numerous Ford pictures are loss-of-family stories), *How Green Was My Valley* could easily have served as an indelible swan song had Ford been killed instead of wounded at the battle of Midway (a record of which was Ford's first of several war documentaries). For his work on *How Green*, Ford won the best director Oscar for the second year in a row (his third in seven years). As

Ford pointed out to me, he was the youngest at a table of thirteen children born to his Irish immigrant parents in Maine, and he clearly empathized with the character of the coal miner's youngest, whom Roddy McDowall as a child of ten so eloquently played. The heartrending emotions of the boy growing up in a family and a way of life that is falling apart are often conveyed in the simplest of moments, as in the one where Roddy's character is left alone at table with his father (a superb portrayal by Donald Crisp) after a family argument, and the boy clears his throat to get an acknowledgment of his presence. No other American picturemaker had the poetic temperament or the innate humanity to so movingly vivify the past, as well as the losing of it.

That Ford and Katharine Hepburn had fallen in love less than five years before and, because Ford was already a married father of two, the romance was never taken to the depth that both wanted, must have contributed heavily to the director's treatment of the forbidden love between the coal miner's only daughter (Maureen O'Hara, incandescent and earthy) and the town's minister (played with great dignity by Walter Pidgeon). The degree of passionate feeling generated for this relationship in *How Green* helps to reveal the intensity of Ford's own feelings at that time. In fact, Ford put himself on active duty immediately after hearing that Hepburn had begun an affair with Spencer Tracy (also Irish, married, and a father). Beyond that, the picture is a metaphor of man's loss of the Garden, as the war threatened to end the entire human family.

I think *How Green Was My Valley*, superbly adapted by screenwriter Philip Dunne, is the best film ever to win the Oscar for best picture, which also makes the disparagement of the Academy's choice over *Citizen Kane* such a poor case. If these two films went up against each other today in the heart of the country, I believe the Academy vote would reflect the public's reaction for two basic reasons: *Kane* is about the rich and privileged, while *How Green* is about everybody else. As Welles himself—an ardent Ford admirer—said to me once, "With Ford at his best, you can feel what the earth is made of." The other reason is hope, which Welles's film doesn't give, but which Ford's does. At the end of *How Green*, the final devastating loss of the father is reprieved from utter gloom by a belief in the survival of the spirit, and then memory-images take us back through the entire story in what is probably the most devastatingly moving finish in pictures. But this was at the peak of the sound era, which saw the greatest number of lasting works released between 1939 and 1942. If there was ever a serious picture to see with the family and friends you love, it is *How Green Was My Valley*. My immigrant parents adored it; they introduced it to me when I was about ten, and it has continued to hold a treasured place in our family's shared experience. Bring plenty of Kleenex.

OTHER JOHN FORD PICTURES:
Four Sons (1928; with Margaret Mann, James Hall).
Arrowsmith (1931; with Ronald Colman, Helen Hayes).
The Informer (1935; with Victor McLaglen).
The Hurricane (1938; with Jon Hall, Dorothy Lamour, Raymond Massey).
Young Mr. Lincoln (1939; with Henry Fonda, Jane Darwell).
They Were Expendable (1945; with Robert Montgomery, John Wayne, Donna Reed).
My Darling Clementine (1946; with Henry Fonda, Victor Mature).

Also see Weeks 11, 22, and 38.

HOLIDAY

I've always had an exceedingly soft spot in my heart for George Cukor's 1938 version of the Philip Barry social comedy, *Holiday*, starring Katharine Hepburn and Cary Grant, both in top form. The first time I saw it was during the Christmas season at what used to be the Alden (at Sixty-seventh Street and Broadway) when I was sixteen years old and the movie was seventeen.

Walking home in the evening, I remember, I was feeling unbelievably happy, euphorically inspired about life's vast potential—all as a result of this wonderful romantic comedy-drama, in its own day not a popular success. It was, in fact, sometime around the release of *Holiday* that exhibitors were calling Ms. Hepburn "box-office poison"—a condition that prevailed until two years later when the indestructible Kate resurrected herself in another Cukor-Barry-Grant collaboration, *The Philadelphia Story* (1940), though by then she had to take second billing to Cary.

However, I've always preferred *Holiday*, the story of a rich family's female black sheep (Hepburn) and her affection for an unorthodox young man (Grant) who believes one should take a long holiday early in life to figure out what the world is all about rather than simply going blindly after the bucks; things are further complicated by the black sheep's conventional sister, who is planning to marry the guy. With a thoroughly marvelous supporting cast, the movie has at least two other memorable performances: Lew Ayres as Hepburn's drunken brother—who tries to but can't quite extricate himself from the staid family traditions— and Edward Everett Horton as Grant's best friend, an underpaid but clearly most intellectual and witty college professor. The screenplay, which is somewhat different from Barry's original, is by that brilliant Algonquin Round Table member Donald Ogden Stewart.

This picture was actually the second of three Cukor-Hepburn-Grant films, the first being the resounding flop *Sylvia Scarlett* (1935), which was not at all a bad film and the first time Grant—playing a cocky Cockney— blossomed as a comic actor. Of course, it was Cukor who discovered Ms. Hepburn for 1932's *A Bill of Divorcement* (opposite John Barrymore) and subsequently directed her— the screen's longest-lived star actor—in eight other movies, the last being an utterly delightful 1975 television film, *Love Among the Ruins,* costarring Laurence Olivier.

The director's remarkably empathetic handling of actors resulted in some of the finest performances of the American screen, including Garbo's *Camille* (1936), her finest dramatic turn. So many of his literate works hold up so well. Though *Holiday* is not among Cukor's most famous works, it remains one of my particular favorites and cannot fail to cheer up the darkest season. Cary Grant even does a couple of gymnastic flips that are wonderfully exhilarating. What more could you want?

OTHER GEORGE CUKOR–KATHARINE HEPBURN–CARY GRANT
PICTURES:

Sylvia Scarlett (1935; with Edmund Gwenn).

The Philadelphia Story (1940; with James Stewart, Ruth
Hussey).

OTHER CUKOR-HEPBURN PICTURES:

See Week 7 and the recommendations that follow that film.

OTHER CUKOR PICTURES:

See Weeks 7 and 35 and the recommendations that follow
those films.

THE SHOP
AROUND THE CORNER

For some reason, end-of-the-year holidays are an especially good time for Ernst Lubitsch movies (see Weeks 12 and 49). Not that there's any time that *isn't* a terrific time for the properly celebrated "Lubitsch Touch": human, witty, economical, ambiguous, simple yet complicated, funny, romantic, oblique, light but profound—in one word, Mozartian. Lubitsch is the director's director. Time after time, when I've talked with other filmmakers, as disparate as Alfred Hitchcock and Howard Hawks, Jean Renoir and Orson Welles, they all said there were many directors—and then there was Lubitsch.

His towering 1940 bittersweet human comedy of vintage genius, *The Shop Around the Corner*, only becomes more precious as the years pass, like the finest wine—Lubitsch's films often supplying a comparably inspiring buzz, but one that stays with you far longer than any wine could. It's also got James Stewart and Margaret Sullavan, for God's sake! There's been a tiny tradition of recycling the wonderful central plot: Two feuding, acrimonious workers are unaware that they are actually secret pen pals. There have been a couple of musical remakes—one on screen (*In the Good Old Summertime*, 1948), one on stage (*She Loves Me*, 1963)— plus 1998's nonmusical movie *You've Got Mail*, which took the main plot but virtually nothing else. And none of these even come close to the special holiday warmth and humanity that emanates from every frame of this original comic masterwork.

Indeed, *The Shop Around the Corner* is one of the richest looks at the oddly contradictory and unpredictably diverse traits of human nature. Set in a pre–World War II Budapest department store called Matuscheck's, and starring three anything-but-Hungarian types—Stewart, Sullavan, and the Wizard of Oz himself, Frank Morgan, as Mr. Matuscheck (all at their absolute best)—the picture never for a second stretches credulity; you soon realize Lubitsch's unspoken point that regular people are the same all over the world, no matter how individually quirky they may be.

As I said, the main plot—that Stewart and Sullavan, who do not at all get along with each other in the workplace, are, without knowing it, pseudonymous pen pals of amazing rapport—is extremely good, but Lubitsch does not lean on it for support. Rather, he nearly throws it away as only the main thread in his tapestry of observations on the lives of all the employees at the shop, as well as the owner, whose plight is actually the most touching: the man's wife (never seen) is having an affair with one of his employees. Supporting players get equal weight in this beautiful movie: the brilliantly obnoxious two-faced clerk Joseph Schildkraut, or the delightfully wiseass delivery boy William Tracy, or the sublimely funny Felix Bressart. When Bressart tells about the boss calling him an idiot, he explains: "I said, 'Yes, Mr. Matuscheck, I'm an idiot.'. . . I'm no fool!" Or when he sets out his philosophy about entertaining friends at his home: "Listen," he says, "if someone is *really* your friend, he comes *after* dinner."

Talking about the supposedly onerous restrictions of the studio system, Jimmy Stewart once said to me, "Nobody ever told Lubitsch what to do!" He made films his own way, and they reflect his wit and wisdom.

The Shop Around the Corner is a picture that makes you feel good about people and life, even while it touches you with the transience of happiness, the pain of regret, the essentially irreconcilable difference between youth and age. Like all great art, it enriches the soul, makes you better through its special glow—one my family has always liked to bask in around Christmastime, maybe because it is one of Lubitsch's greatest gifts to us.

OTHER ERNST LUBITSCH PICTURES:
  See Weeks 12 and 49—and the recommendations that follow those films.

ACKNOWLEDGMENTS

First of all, my warmest thanks to Iris Chester, who typed all these pieces in their various forms, and who helped so much to organize and shape the material, as she has with everything I've written since 1981. And to William Peiffer, long my business associate, who saw to it that so many things kept going in all areas, while this and other matters were brought to fruition, my continuing gratitude. The encouragement and loyalty of these two people have been extremely fortifying.

Since this book is the product of my return to New York in early 1997—after having resided in Los Angeles for three decades—I would also like to acknowledge those people who most helped me in my homecoming. Filmmaker Henry Jaglom gave me enormous assistance in the first year; we have been friends since we both lived in Manhattan— knew each other's parents—and over the years he has been instrumental in several key transitions for me; all the time, he's been a pal, never more so than during this most recent metamorphosis. My enduring thanks go to him.

As they do to the courageous and conscientious film distributor-exhibitor-producer Daniel Talbot, in whose revolutionary Sixties revival house, the New Yorker, I saw quite a few of the pictures in this book for the first time. He has been a heartening, giving presence in my life for four decades, and he generously helped in this recent move. Both he and his lovely wife, Toby, have meant a lot to me. There is no way to repay such debts.

My old pal, superpublicist extraordinaire Bobby Zarem, who has done me many favors over the years, introduced my wife, Louise, to entrepreneur Bryan Bantry, and he befriended her and then was amazingly generous to both of us with his time and hospitality in the often rocky move back to New York; I cannot thank him enough for his countless gestures of selfless aid. In my experience, his magnanimity was unique. His entire staff was also remarkably helpful, but especially Margo MacNabb, who at that juncture worked for Bryan, and went out of her way numerous times for months with any number of secretarial tasks that made life so much easier; big thanks go to her. Also to the others at Bryan's, especially: Bob Felner, Lisa Raydon, Elizabeth Houghton, Pam La Belle, Palma and Marisa Driscoll.

As I said in the introduction, *The New York Observer*'s editor in chief Peter Kaplan, with whom I had worked on a screenplay in the mid-1980s, had the idea of my doing a weekly column for him on older films, and this had a wonderfully positive effect on my return to Manhattan; I deeply appreciate his enthusiastic endorsement and the space he offered. Also, the *Observer*'s publisher, Arthur Carter, welcomed me into his home and introduced me to a number of his friends who helped us into the city in important ways; my warmest thanks to him and particularly to Sandy Leiberman, who was instrumental in connecting us to an apartment.

Of course, it was Victoria Wilson, the brilliant executive editor at Knopf, who gave me the central piece of advice in my homecoming. She had been my editor on the well-received 1997 book of interviews I did with directors, *Who the Devil Made It,* and she said: "Move to New York and let the book come out." Everything else, she felt, would flow from that. She was correct. It was she, also, who first presented these pieces to Ballantine's associate publisher Joe Blades as a possible book, so Vicky has at least triple thanks coming, and she is a real friend, too.

I have already noted in the introduction my debt to Joe Blades, who provided the idea for this book's organization. And the process of making it a reality with Joe, from inception to manuscript to line editing, copy editing, photo selection, galleys, etc., has been an unmitigated pleasure. Not only is he a real professional, but his encouragement is galvanizing.

At the Museum of Modern Art Film Library I thank profusely Mary Lea Bandy, Laurence Kardish, and Joshua Siegel, all of whom have welcomed me back to that great institution (which published my first three monographs in the Sixties), giving me another prestigious and exemplary place from which to communicate my popularizing of movies I like. And all three of these people are themselves so likable, it's a pleasure to work with them. My thanks as well to Paolo Cherchi Usai, film curator at the legendary George Eastman House in Rochester, NY, who paid me a lovely tribute and helped us out enormously with archival storage.

Another who has generously helped me back with friendship and advice is producer Julian Schlossberg, an old and valued friend, who introduced me to financial adviser Ken Starr (no relation to the Clinton accuser); Ken has been kind and most helpful in a number of important ways.

My pal Zack Norman has my thanks for his continuing support and for setting me up with his friend Harry Sandler of the American Program Bureau; Harry and his associates, including their most amicable boss, Bob Walker, have all been most forthcoming and set up a lot of terrific speaking engagements that also helped the transition to a new life in

New York City. Zack also connected me to the amazing Sheldon Abend, who pulled together some projects for me, and has become a friend and working associate I value.

At Photofest, Joe McElhaney, and at the Kobal Collection, Bob Costenza, have both been extremely thorough and helpful in finding photos for the book. Many thanks to them.

Though the majority of the movies in this book were made on the West Coast, almost all of this writing was done two blocks from New York's oldest school, Collegiate, where I attended classes for twelve years, just a few blocks from where I lived until I was thirteen and then another few blocks the other way from where I lived until leaving for California. The perfect spot, as far as I'm concerned, for a new beginning. And I am indebted to all the people I've mentioned above for helping to bring that about. Also, as the Cole Porter song goes, "I Happen to Like New York."

INDEX

(The Recommendations that follow each week have not been indexed.)

ABOUT THE AUTHOR

PETER BOGDANOVICH is the author of numerous books, including *This Is Orson Welles, John Ford,* and most recently, *Who the Devil Made It,* his bestselling chronicle of sixteen pioneering filmmakers. Bogdanovich is also a film director, screenwriter, actor, and producer whose works for the screen include *The Last Picture Show, What's Up, Doc?, Paper Moon, Mask, Texasville, They All Laughed, Saint Jack, Daisy Miller,* and *Noises Off.* He lives in New York City.

If you enjoyed this book,
don't miss Peter Bogdanovich's masterpiece,
a collection of his conversations with legendary film directors:

• Robert Aldrich • George Cukor • Allan Dwan • Howard Hawks
• Alfred Hitchcock • Chuck Jones • Fritz Lang • Joseph H. Lewis
• Sidney Lumet • Leo McCarey • Otto Preminger • Don Siegel
• Josef von Sternberg • Frank Tashlin • Edgar G. Ulmer • Raoul Walsh

"A HUGE AND VALUABLE BOOK . . . BOGDANOVICH
INCLUDES EVERYTHING: HISTORY, TECHNIQUE, GOSSIP,
MINUTIAE."
—Roger Ebert, *The New York Times Book Review*

"A MUST READ FOR ANY FILM NUT."
—*Details*

More critical acclaim for *WHO THE DEVIL MADE IT*
by Peter Bogdanovich

"A RARE PEEK AT THE NUTS AND BOLTS OF THE
MOVIEMAKING BUSINESS . . . Bogdanovich gets Hawks to
explain how he kept an insouciant Katharine Hepburn in line by
threatening to 'kick [her] behind' in *Bringing Up Baby*. . . . Hitchcock
derides the 'front office' that can't understand why Janet Leigh would
be killed off so early in *Psycho*. . . . Siegel is furious about execs who
insisted on grafting their own opening and ending onto 1956's
Invasion of the Body Snatchers. . . . Delightful . . . Eloquent."
—*Entertainment Weekly*

"ENLIGHTENING . . . His remarkable access, conversational
method of interviewing, and status as a peer in the industry provoked
[these directors] to describe in detail their motivations, methods, and
madnesses in making the most memorable movies
of the twentieth century."
—*The Washington Post Book World*

"CHOCKABLOCK WITH ODD FACTS AND FASCINATING
ANECDOTES . . . The interviews . . . encompass nearly the entire
span of motion picture history."
—*Los Angeles Times*

"ABSORBING."
—*Newsweek*